MEN'S MANUAL

"...When the enemy shall come in like a flood, the Spirit of the Lord shall lift up a standard against him" (Isaiah 59:19).

2

Institute in Basic Youth Conflicts

MEN'S MANUAL

"And he shall turn the heart of the fathers to the children, and the heart of the children to their fathers, lest I come and smite the earth with a curse" (Malachi 4:6).

INSTITUTE IN BASIC YOUTH CONFLICTS, INC.   BOX ONE   OAK BROOK, ILLINOIS 60521

GOD'S JUDGMENT WHEN MEN FAIL
TO BE SPIRITUAL LEADERS...

"...The child shall behave himself proudly against the ancient, and the base against the honorable" (Isaiah 3:5).

"...Children are their oppressors, and women rule[1] over them..." (Isaiah 3:12).

1. Hebrew: Mâshal: Rule; used to imply domination.

HOW TO USE THIS MANUAL

☐ **1. READ PART FIVE FIRST**

The only way to effectively build Godly character and Scriptural convictions in your personal life, marriage, and family is to be kind and loving in all that you do (pp. 132-139).

☐ **2. LIST YOUR CHARACTER QUALITY PRIORITY**

Ask each one in your family to number the following qualities from one to ten on the basis of their importance to a successful family. Follow further instructions on pages 18-19.

Quality	Wife's Priority (Number from 1-10)	Son's and Daughter's Priority (Number from 1-10)				Add Numbers Together	Priority List (Lowest total first)
ATTENTIVENESS	8	☐	☐	☐	☐	_____	_____
OBEDIENCE	3	☐	☐	☐	☐	_____	_____
TRUTHFULNESS	9	☐	☐	☐	☐	_____	_____
PUNCTUALITY	10	☐	☐	☐	☐	_____	_____
NEATNESS	☐	☐	☐	☐	☐	_____	_____
GRATEFULNESS	6	☐	☐	☐	☐	_____	_____
LOYALTY	4	☐	☐	☐	☐	_____	_____
PATIENCE	5	☐	☐	☐	☐	_____	_____
FORGIVENESS	☐	☐	☐	☐	☐	_____	_____
RESPECTFULNESS	1	☐	☐	☐	☐	_____	_____

All Scripture references are from the King James Version of the Bible, unless otherwise noted.

Printed in the United States of America.

ISBN 0-916888-04-5

Library of Congress
Catalog Card Number: 79-88994

☐ **3. SET UP "SHARING TIMES" WITH YOUR WIFE**

The key to a successful marriage and family is intimate communication. Set up a regular time each week when you and your wife can meet to define, identify, and develop Godly character in your lives, marriage, and family. See instructions on pages 18-19.

☐ **4. ESTABLISH "SHARING TIMES" WITH YOUR FAMILY**

Set aside one mealtime each week when the family can work on the quiz placemats and discuss basic principles, Godly character, and Scriptural convictions. See instructions on pages 18-21.

☐ ● **STUDY FURTHER INSTRUCTIONS ON PAGES 18-21**

TABLE OF CONTENTS

WHY DO CHILDREN REBEL?

CAUSE	EFFECT
☐ When a father does not fulfill promises...	His children get wounded spirits.
☐ When a father does not admit he is wrong...	His children lose confidence in his leadership.
☐ When a father refuses to ask for forgiveness...	His children react to his pride.
☐ When a father does not have right priorities...	His children feel that he is too busy for them.
☐ When a father is too strict in discipline...	His children have their spirits broken.
☐ When a father gives too much freedom to his children...	His children see freedom as a form of rejection.
☐ When a father neglects his parents...	His children do not honor the counsel of their grandparents.
☐ When a father puts his parents in a nursing home for the sake of convenience...	His children are taught to reject older people.
☐ When a father does not love his wife...	His children take up offenses for their mother.
☐ When a father neglects God's Word...	His children reject the authority of God and the Bible.
☐ When a father sacrifices his family for a better retirement...	His children develop a temporal value system.
☐ When a father disciplines in anger...	His children have seeds of bitterness.
☐ When a father delegates his children's education to others...	His children cease to respect him as a teacher.
☐ When a father does not teach his children how to please him...	His children feel frustrated and rejected.
☐ When a father focuses on the outward beauty of others...	His children feel inferior and reject themselves.
☐ When a father is impatient with his children...	His children seek approval from friends.
☐ When a father has inconsistent standards...	His children despise him.
☐ When a father tries to warn his children only of the consequences of sin...	His children are challenged to be successful in avoiding the consequences.
☐ When a father lets his wife assume spiritual leadership...	His children may regard religion as childish when they grow older.
☐ When a father does not have personal convictions...	His children accept situational ethics and excuse in excess what their father allowed in moderation.

WHY DO WIVES REACT?

CAUSE	EFFECT
☐ When a husband fails to be a spiritual leader...	His wife feels insecure.
☐ When a husband allows problems to continue and even get worse...	His wife feels helpless and finally takes matters into her own hands.
☐ When a husband does not support his wife in disciplining the children...	His wife blames him for rebellious children.
☐ When a husband spends extra money on things which he enjoys...	His wife resents the financial pressure under which they must live.
☐ When a husband does not accept himself...	His wife feels the same rejection from him.
☐ When a husband praises or admires other women...	His wife feels inferior and jealous.
☐ When a husband verbalizes love only when he wants a physical relationship with his wife...	His wife feels degraded and used and finds it hard to love him.
☐ When a husband forgets anniversaries and other special occasions...	His wife feels that she is unimportant and not cherished by him.
☐ When a husband does not praise his wife for specific things...	His wife feels frustrated in not knowing how to please him.
☐ When a husband does not spend time talking with his wife...	His wife finds others who will listen to her true feelings.
☐ When a husband fails to notice the little extra things his wife does for him...	His wife loses her creativity for her husband and their home and looks for outside interests.
☐ When a husband makes bad judgments and unwise business decisions...	His wife resists his will in future decisions.
☐ When a husband is not alert to dangers which his wife faces...	His wife feels unprotected.
☐ When a husband neglects needed home repairs...	His wife builds up resentment and impatience.
☐ When a husband does not have good manners or consistent manners...	His wife loses self-worth and feels isolated from her husband's real world.
☐ When a husband lusts after other women...	His wife feels inadequate in trying to meet her husband's physical needs.
☐ When a husband loses his temper and does not ask for forgiveness...	His wife reacts to his pride.

ANOTHER REASON WHY WIVES REACT

BEFORE ADAM AND EVE SINNED:

1. GOD ESTABLISHED THE HUSBAND'S HEADSHIP

God created man first and gave him tasks to perform; then God created the woman:"...I will make him an help meet for him." The Hebrew word for "help" means "to aid" or "to assist."

If Eve was created "to aid" Adam, it is logically assumed that Adam was to have had the leadership position. He had to provide direction, or his wife would not have known how to aid or assist him.

2. GOD ESTABLISHED THE WIFE'S SUBMISSION

Before Adam and Eve sinned, Eve was in submission to Adam. This is clearly indicated by Scripture. In order for Eve to have fulfilled her function as an aid or assistant, she would have had to be in submission to the one whom she was aiding. The purpose and submission of the woman in God's creation order is reaffirmed in I Corinthians 11:3-10.

AFTER ADAM AND EVE SINNED:

1. THE WIFE'S WILLING SUBMISSION WAS CORRUPTED

God said to Eve, "...Thy desire shall be to thy husband, and he shall rule over thee."[2] In the Hebrew, the two clauses in this sentence are in direct opposition. The first clause is in tension with the second clause. The literal meaning is, "thy desire shall be to [control] thy husband... "

This same sentence structure is used in Genesis 4:7. God is telling Cain that sin shall "desire" to control him but he must "rule over" it.

The Fall marked the beginning of the conflict over the headship of the family. No longer does the husband rule easily. He must work to retain his headship. Thus, the New Testament commands the wife to submit to her husband.[3]

2. THE HUSBAND'S LOVING LEADERSHIP WAS CORRUPTED

As a result of the Fall, man has a corrupted desire for complete, unchallenged authority. This desire violates the purpose of love and destroys the marriage relationship. Thus, the New Testament commands the husband to love his wife as Christ loved the Church.[4]

3. GOD CONFIRMED THE HUSBAND'S HEADSHIP

God said to the woman, "...Thy desire shall be to [control] thy husband, and he shall rule over thee." The husband is to exercise headship, but he is to do it with wisdom, patience, and love.[5]

1. Genesis 2:18.
2. Genesis 3:16.
3. Ephesians 5:22; I Peter 3:1.
4. Ephesians 5:25.
5. I Corinthians 11:3, I Peter 3:7. Ephesians 5:23.

WHAT IF A FATHER HAS ALREADY FAILED?

A MAN WHO FAILS IS NOT A FAILURE

A man who fails and gives up is a failure! However, God promises "beauty for ashes."[1] God allows us to fail when we try to succeed in our own strength. His most powerful illustrations have been in the lives of men who knew their own weaknesses but learned how to draw upon God's strength.[2]

FAILURE LEAVES "SCARS," BUT THESE "SCARS" CAN BE TURNED INTO GOD'S GLORY FOR SONS AND DAUGHTERS

Disobedience always results in loss and regret. When the nation of Israel disobeyed God, He scattered the families and destroyed the temple. Later, the people repented and rebuilt the temple, but it was less glorious than the original structure. However, God promised to make it more glorious than the former temple if they would be obedient to Him.[3]

THE DREAMS OF FATHERS ARE OFTEN FULFILLED BY THEIR SONS AND DAUGHTERS

Children tend to adopt their father's values. If his chief concern is for temporal things, theirs will often be also. However, children may take a different approach to temporal things. If, for example, a father is overly concerned about retirement, his son may be slothful on the basis that if retirement is so important, he will beat his father to it.

When sons and daughters adopt their father's God-given goals, the father can provide much-needed encouragement, resources, and counsel for these goals. This was illustrated in the building of the temple. David had the vision for it, but his son built it.

THE SINS OF FATHERS ARE PASSED ON TO THE THIRD AND FOURTH GENERATION

A father must be a rebuilder, no matter what his past failures may have been. His sins tend to recur in the lives of his sons and daughters. The manifestations may differ, but the basic failure will be there.

When sons and daughters react to their father, they become just like him either in actions, or attitudes, or both.

What fathers allow in moderation, their sons and daughters tend to excuse in excess.

1. Isaiah 61:3-4: "...To give unto them beauty for ashes, the oil of joy for mourning... and they shall repair the waste cities, the desolations of many generations."
2. II Corinthians 12:9: "...For my strength is made perfect in weakness...."
3. Haggai 2:3-9.

KING DAVID

David failed, but he was not a failure. He had a desire to build a great temple for God, but God would not let him build it.

SOLOMON

David's son, Solomon, built the temple, but he was greatly assisted by the tremendous provisions and contacts which his father had prepared for him.

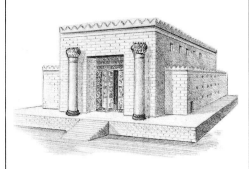

SOLOMON'S TEMPLE

The original temple was a breathtaking sight. However, when the nation sinned, God destroyed the temple. When they repented, God gave them the desire and the power to rebuild the temple, but it was less glorious.

WHAT IS THE PURPOSE OF THIS MANUAL?

FOR FATHERS:

● This manual is designed to pinpoint the basic Scriptural convictions which a father must have in order to prevent rebellion in his children and reaction from his wife. Precise steps of action are given on how to establish and maintain these convictions in personal living, marriage, family, and business.

● The purpose of this manual is to give fathers a basic guide by which they can train their sons and daughters to be wise in God's Word and mighty in God's Spirit. So much of the education of our day is not founded on basic principles of Scripture, nor is it teaching or reinforcing Scriptural convictions. Instead, it is undermining the very foundation of Godly wisdom and character. The time has come for fathers to reclaim the primary responsibility and the direction for teaching their own sons and daughters.

● The Scriptural authority for a father to teach his sons and daughters is clearly established: "And these words...shall be in thine heart: And thou shalt teach them diligently unto thy children...."[1] "...A child...is under tutors and governors until the time appointed of the father."[2]

FOR GRANDFATHERS:

● A father's responsibility for his sons and daughters does not end when they finish their education or when they are married. His responsibility continues when he becomes a grandfather and for as long as he lives.

● God knows that the strength and stability of a family depend on the wisdom and dedication of the grandfather. Thus, He commands grandfathers to remember the principles and ways of God and to "...teach them [to] thy sons, and thy sons' sons."[3]

● The time has come for grandfathers to renew their responsibility and commitment to their families and to work with each family member on the basis of Scriptural principles and convictions.

● When the hearts of fathers and grandfathers are turned toward their own sons and daughters, we will raise up the foundations of many Godly generations[4] and escape the judgment of God upon our nation.[5]

1. Deuteronomy 6:6-7.   4. Isaiah 61:1-4.
2. Galatians 4:1-2.   5. Malachi 4:6.
3. Deuteronomy 4:9.

HOW DO CONVICTIONS DIFFER FROM PREFERENCES?

QUIZ:

WHICH ARE CONVICTIONS, AND WHICH ARE PREFERENCES?

		CONVICTION	PREFERENCE
1.	I have a conviction that I should try to overcome a drinking problem.	☐	☐
2.	I have a conviction that a man should lead his family, but in some situations this may change.	☐	☐
3.	I have a conviction that some of the television programs that I watch are harmful for my children.	☐	☐
4.	I have a conviction that I should not pay taxes to programs which violate God's Word.	☐	☐

ANSWERS:

1. A preference—not a conviction. A conviction must be seen in daily living.

2. A preference—not a conviction. A conviction must not change.

3. A preference—not a conviction. A conviction must be consistent. If the television programs are harmful for children, they are also harmful for adults.

4. An unscriptural conviction. Jesus paid taxes to the very government which put Him to death, and God commands us to pay all of our taxes (Romans 13:6-7).

TEN SCRIPTURAL CONVICTIONS

...which every man must teach his family in order to protect them from the destructive influences of wrong desires, false philosophies, and Satanic temptations.

1. God alone is sovereign, and the Bible is His inspired Word and the final authority for my life.

2. My purpose in life is to seek God with my whole heart and to build my goals around His priorities.

3. My body is the living temple of God and must not be defiled by the lusts of the world.

4. My church must teach the foundational truths of the Bible and reinforce my basic convictions.

5. My children and grandchildren belong to God, and it is my responsibility to teach them Scriptural principles, Godly character, and basic convictions.

6. My activities must never weaken the Scriptural convictions of another Christian.

7. My marriage is a life-long commitment to God and to my marriage partner.

8. My money is a trust from God and must be earned and managed according to Scriptural principles.

9. My words must be in harmony with God's Word, especially when reproving and restoring a Christian brother.

10. My affections must be set on things above, not on things in the earth.

QUESTION:

CAN YOU IDENTIFY THE SCRIPTURAL BASIS OF THESE TEN CONVICTIONS?

CONVICTIONS	OLD TESTAMENT BASIS	NEW TESTAMENT BASIS
1. The Bible is the inspired Word of God and the final authority for my life.	First Commandment: "Thou shalt have no other gods before me" (Exodus 20:3). (Rejecting inspiration makes a god of our intellect.) David's Teaching: "...Thou hast magnified thy word above all thy name" (Psalm 138:2).	Christ's Teaching: "...Man shall not live by bread alone, but by every word that proceedeth out of the mouth of God" (Matthew 4:4). Paul's Teaching: "All Scripture is given by inspiration of God..." (II Timothy 3:16).
2. My purpose in life is to seek God with my whole heart and to build my goals around His priorities.	Second Commandment: "Thou shalt not make unto thee any graven image... nor serve them... " (Exodus 20:4-5). David's Teaching: "Blessed are they that keep his testimonies, and that seek him with the whole heart" (Psalm 119:2).	Christ's Teaching: "But seek ye first the kingdom of God, and his righteousness: and all these things shall be added unto you" (Matthew 6:33). Paul's Teaching: "...I count all things but loss for the excellency of the knowledge of Christ..." (Philippians 3:8).
3. My body is the living temple of God and must not be defiled by the lusts of the world.	Third Commandment: "Thou shalt not take the name of the Lord thy God in vain..." (Exodus 20:7). (We damage His name by immorality.) Nathan's Reproof of David's Immorality: "...By this deed thou hast given great occasion to the enemies of the Lord to blaspheme..." (II Samuel 12:14). Daniel's Example: "But Daniel purposed in his heart that he would not defile himself..." (Daniel 1:8).	Christ's Teaching: "For from within, out of the heart of men, proceed evil thoughts, adulteries, fornications... and defile the man" (Mark 7:21-23). Paul's Teaching: "Know ye not that ye are the temple of God...if any man defile the temple of God, him shall God destroy... " (I Corinthians 3:16-17). Peter's Teaching: "...Abstain from fleshly lusts, which war against the soul" (I Peter 2:11).
4. My church must teach the foundational truths of Scripture and reinforce my basic convictions.	Fourth Commandment: "Remember the sabbath day, to keep it holy" (Exodus 20:8). God's Promise: "If my people, which are called by my name, shall humble themselves, and pray, and seek my face, and turn from their wicked ways; then will I hear from heaven, and will forgive their sin, and will heal their land" (II Chronicles 7:14). David's Teaching: "Give unto the Lord the glory due unto his name; worship the Lord in the beauty of holiness" (Psalm 29:2).	Christ's Teaching: "Beware of false prophets, which come to you in sheep's clothing, but inwardly they are ravening wolves: Ye shall know them by their fruits... " (Matthew 7:15-16). Paul's Teaching: "...What fellowship hath righteousness with unrighteousness? and what communion hath light with darkness... Wherefore come out from among them, and be ye separate, saith the Lord..." (II Corinthians 6:14-17). Peter's Teaching: "For the time is come that judgment must begin at the house of God..." (I Peter 4:17).

CONVICTIONS	OLD TESTAMENT BASIS	NEW TESTAMENT BASIS
5. My children and grandchildren belong to God, and it is my responsibility to teach them Scriptural principles, Godly character, and basic convictions.	Fifth Commandment: "Honor thy father and thy mother..." (Exodus 20:12). (A child's honor permits a father to teach.) God's Instruction: "And these words, which I command thee this day, shall be in thine heart: And thou shalt teach them diligently unto thy children..." (Deuteronomy 6:6,7). "...Teach them [to] thy sons, and thy sons' sons" (Deuteronomy 4:9). David's Teaching: "Lo, children are an heritage of the Lord: and the fruit of the womb is his reward" (Psalm 127:3).	Christ's Teaching: "...Suffer little children, and forbid them not, to come unto me: for of such is the kingdom of heaven" (Matthew 19:14). Paul's Teaching: "[A child]...is under tutors and governors until the time appointed of the father" (Galatians 4:1,2). "...We exhorted and comforted and charged every one of you, as a father doth his children" (I Thessalonians 2:11).
6. My activities must never weaken the Scriptural convictions of another Christian.	Sixth Commandment: "Thou shalt not kill" (Exodus 20:13). (This can also be applied in a spiritual sense.) Solomon's Warning: "Whoso causeth the righteous to go astray in an evil way, he shall fall himself into his own pit..." (Proverbs 28:10).	Christ's Warning: "But whoso shall offend one of these little ones which believe in me, it were better for him that a millstone were hanged about his neck, and that he were drowned in the depth of the sea" (Matthew 18:6). Paul's Teaching: "...But judge this rather, that no man put a stumbling-block or an occasion to fall in his brother's way" (Romans 14:13).
7. My marriage is a lifelong commitment to God and to my marriage partner.	Seventh Commandment: "Thou shalt not commit adultery" (Exodus 20:14). God's Creation Purpose: "Therefore shall a man leave his father and his mother, and shall cleave unto his wife: and they shall be one flesh" (Genesis 2:24). Solomon's Warning: "...Whoso committeth adultery with a woman lacketh understanding: he that doeth it destroyeth his own soul" (Proverbs 6:32).	Christ's Teaching: "...What therefore God hath joined together, let not man put asunder" (Matthew 19:6). Paul's Teaching: "For the woman which hath an husband is bound by the law to her husband so long as he liveth; but if the husband be dead, she is loosed from the law of her husband. So then if, while her husband liveth, she be married to another man, she shall be called an adulteress..." (Romans 7:2,3).
8. My money is a trust from God and must be earned and managed according to Scriptural principles.	Eighth Commandment: "Thou shalt not steal" (Exodus 20:15). God's Instruction: "Thou shalt remember the Lord thy God: for it is he that giveth thee power to get wealth..." (Deuteronomy 8:18). Solomon's Warning: "...In the revenues of the wicked is trouble" (Proverbs 15:6). Malachi's Warning: "Will a man rob God? Yet ye have robbed me...In tithes and offerings" (Malachi 3:8).	Christ's Teaching: "If therefore ye have not been faithful in the unrighteous mammon [riches], who will commit to your trust the true riches?" (Luke 16:11). Paul's Teaching: "For the love of money is the root of all evil: which while some coveted after, they have erred from the faith, and pierced themselves through with many sorrows" (I Timothy 6:10).

CONVICTIONS	OLD TESTAMENT BASIS	NEW TESTAMENT BASIS
9. **My words must be in harmony with Scripture, especially when reproving and restoring a Christian brother.**	Ninth Commandment: "Thou shalt not bear false witness against thy neighbor" (Exodus 20:16). Solomon's Instruction: "The heart of the righteous studieth to answer..." (Proverbs 15:28). "Death and life are in the power of the tongue..." (Proverbs 18:21). "Debate thy cause with thy neighbor himself; and discover not a secret to another" (Proverbs 25:9).	Christ's Teaching: "For by thy words thou shalt be justified, and by thy words thou shalt be condemned" (Matthew 12:37). "Moreover if thy brother shall trespass against thee, go and tell him his fault between thee and him alone" (Matthew 18:15). Paul's Teaching: "Brethren, if a man be overtaken in a fault, ye which are spiritual, restore such an one..." (Galatians 6:1).
10. **My affections must be set on things above, not on things in the earth.**	Tenth Commandment: "Thou shalt not covet thy neighbor's house...nor anything that is thy neighbor's" (Exodus 20:17). Job's Testimony: "...The Lord gave, and the Lord hath taken away; blessed be the name of the Lord" (Job 1:21).	Christ's Teaching: "But lay up for yourselves treasures in heaven...for where your treasure is, there will your heart be also" (Matthew 6:20-21). Paul's Teaching: "Set your affection on things above, not on things on the earth" (Colossians 3:2).

Building a conviction is like growing a tree. It takes the right seed, time, and balanced care—especially in the beginning! Too much sunlight, too much water, or not enough protection, and the tree will die.

It is for this reason that the five commands of I Corinthians 16:13 and 14 are so necessary for a man in order to be successful in building convictions into his own life and into the lives of those in his family.

These commands are actually five steps that every man can follow in order to insure consistency and balance in building convictions. If one step is emphasized too strongly, his wife and children will either react to a conviction, or be out of balance in their own approach to it.

1. Be alert to spiritual danger!
2. Be true to God's standards!
3. Be a man!
4. Be strong!
5. Be kind and loving in all that you do!

HOW TO USE THIS MANUAL

- **REVIEW INITIAL STEPS ON PAGE 6.**

5. KNOW THE SPIRITUAL CONDITION OF EACH FAMILY MEMBER

A wise father will diligently discern whether each member of his family is a Christian and how far each one has progressed in his or her walk with the Lord. (See material on pages 111 and 118.)

6. READ THROUGH THE ENTIRE MANUAL

A quick reading of the entire manual will give you a valuable overview of its scope and outline.

7. GIVE YOUR FAMILY A "CAUSE" TO LIVE FOR!

A person without a cause is like a car without a steering wheel. A person with a cause has the motivation for learning and the basis of discipline and sacrifice. A family with a cause is a family with unity and fellowship.

The cause which every Christian must understand and be committed to is the continuous conflict against the deception and destruction of Satan. We must "put on the whole armour of God, that [we] may be able to stand against the wiles of the devil" (Ephesians 6:11). This is a life and death struggle for individuals, marriages, families, churches, schools, businesses, and governments.

Satan's "lie" to every person is that he or she can be like gods in deciding between what is good and what is evil. When any person depends on his own reasoning, Satan wins.

The cause of a dynamic family is to learn God's principles and become mighty in Spirit so that each member can effectively cast down false reasonings and bring "...every thought to the obedience of Christ" (II Corinthians 10:4-5).

Winning this cause means leading friends and neighbors to salvation and helping fellow Christians grow to spiritual maturity (Colossians 1:28-29).

8. PURPOSE TO LIVE BY SCRIPTURAL CONVICTIONS

This volume amplifies the first of ten convictions. These convictions are listed on page 14 and are essential for the success of every life, marriage, family, church, school, business, and nation. To the degree that any one is violated, there will be corresponding consequences not only in this generation but in generations to come (Exodus 20:5-6).

Begin on page 32 and complete the projects listed for each week. Rearrange your priorities in order to maintain the sharing sessions with your wife and family and to complete this first course in thirty weeks.

9. PURPOSE TO DEVELOP GODLY CHARACTER

The weekly sharing session that you establish with your wife will be for the purpose of defining, identifying, and developing Godly character qualities in your personal life, marriage, family, and business (see page 123).

FIRST WEEK: DEFINE CHARACTER QUALITY No. 1

Quality No. 1 is the quality on page 6 that your family determines was the greatest priority for a successful family. Study this quality on your own and ask your wife to do the same. Look up the word in the dictionary and all the Scripture verses which contain the word or idea. Write down what you find. List examples of men and women in the Bible who had this quality or who violated it. Give present day illustrations of it in as many areas as you can.

FIRST SHARING SESSION:

Combine the definitions, examples, and illustrations which you both learned in your own studies. Ask your wife to record this in a character notebook. Do further study and discussion and conclude your time with prayer. Each one pray for God to build this quality in your life in a deeper way.

SECOND WEEK: IDENTIFY CHARACTER QUALITY No. 1

Look for examples in which your wife or other family members demonstrated this quality. Write them down. Ask your wife to write down examples also.

SECOND SHARING SESSION:

Use the following four questions as the basis of you and your wife writing a letter to each other.

1. Specific ways in which you demonstrated _____(quality)_____ .
2. My inward emotions when you demonstrated _____(quality)_____ .
3. My outward response when you demonstrate _____(quality)_____ .
4. What God is teaching me when you demonstrate _____(quality)_____ .

Exchange your letters. Discuss them and conclude in a time of praying for each other and thanking God for each other.

THIRD WEEK:

Think of projects and ideas which would help you and your family to build this quality in daily living. Projects could include verses to memorize, character drills, books and library films which illustrate the quality, clipping newspaper stories which illustrate the quality or its violation.

THIRD SHARING SESSION:

Share with each other the ideas that you had and work out a way to initiate them in your marriage and family and in training sessions for others.

HOW TO USE QUIZ QUESTIONS TO CREATE INTEREST

> Christ used curiosity to teach vital truths. We would do well to follow His example! These guidelines are important for a father to follow in building curiosity.

BE EXCITED ABOUT WHAT YOU ARE GOING TO TEACH

The word *"enthus"* means "of God." As Christians, we ought to be the most enthusiastic people in the world, especially when sharing the eternal truths of God's Word. A sense of enthusiasm will be communicated as we realize that the material that is to be taught is the most important truth that could be learned. The true basis of enthusiasm, however, is knowing that the material has already become a vital part of our lives.

CREATE INTEREST IN WHAT YOU WANT TO SAY

Scripture uses the example of "breaking up the fallow ground." It illustrates the need to prepare the mind and the heart for the seeds of truth which will be planted in them. This means winning the full attention and interest of the listener.

A. People of all ages usually enjoy demonstrating their knowledge in answering a question. The quiz questions were designed for this purpose. An opening phrase might be, "Let's see if you know the answer to this question."

B. Emphasize that although the question is not easy, they may know the answer.

C. You may want to illustrate the value of knowing God's Word by offering a prize to the one who gives the right answer. If the prize is one that every listener wants, it will certainly build interest in the quiz question. One possibility would be, "The first person who gives the right answer will win a dollar."

D. Pause until everyone is ready to concentrate on the question. Allow interest to build while you patiently wait for everyone's attention. Arrange for dinner tasks that might be distractions to be taken care of first.

CONCENTRATE ON BEING FAIR

Children have a keen ability to sense when someone is being unfair. If they do not sense fairness, they will not only lose interest in the quiz, they will react to it.

A. Become familiar with the question beforehand so that you can clearly and accurately read it. Pronounce each word and read it slowly.

B. Give rules on how the listener should respond before you ask the question: "If you think you know the right answer, raise your hand, and wait until I call on you."

C. Be prepared to see whose hand is raised first. If you cannot watch their response and read the question too, ask someone else to help you determine whose hand goes up first.

D. Allow an equal opportunity to younger members of the family, or to those who do not have as much Bible knowledge, by occasionally saying, "This time let's give the younger members of the family an opportunity to answer first. If they can't answer it, we'll let the rest of the family try."

4. WELCOME AND ENCOURAGE EVERY RESPONSE THAT IS GIVEN

The purpose of the quiz is to encourage as much participation as possible. A negative reaction to an answer will discourage the person and may cause him to feel that you are rejecting him.

A. Think about each answer for a moment or two before indicating whether it is right or wrong. This builds suspense and adds to the interest. It also demonstrates worth to the person and to the thoughts he has given.

B. If a wrong answer is given, do not say, "You're wrong," or "That's a silly answer." Rather, say positively, "That's a good try."

C. Use gentleness and a kind smile when you must inform a person that his answer is "not quite right."

D. Remember that some questions could possibly fit more than one answer. Usually, one is the best answer, but this may not always be true. Because of this, be ready to say, "That could possibly fit, but that is not the best answer to this question."

5. REPEAT THE QUESTION WHEN NECESSARY

If no one guesses the correct answer, which may often be the case, or if there is a long silence, repeat the question. If someone asks you to repeat the question, make sure that you do not overlook those who are waiting to give an answer.

6. GIVE PROPER WARNING BEFORE ENDING THE QUIZ

After giving sufficient time for each person to answer, prepare to end the quiz. You might do this by saying, "You have ten seconds left to give the answer." Make it clear that when you end, the prize can no longer be earned for this quiz.

7. GIVE PROPER RECOGNITION TO THE WINNER

Show genuine enthusiasm for the one who guesses the right answer. Encourage others to share in his happiness. Give the prize immediately after reading the answer.

8. DO NOT GIVE THE ANSWER IF NO ONE GUESSES IT

Each quiz question has been designed for a purpose. Interest in the questions will add enthusiasm to the quiz. It will also allow for comments and questions which may prompt significant further discussion.

9. END ON A HIGH POINT OF INTEREST

Never force a discussion or continue a discussion when the listeners have lost interest. The skill of a good teacher is knowing when to end a discussion. The perfect time is when the listeners have something of importance to think about and interest is high enough for them to want to do it again in the future.

WHY DID IT HAPPEN?

Samson was given supernatural strength, yet he was conquered by a woman, blinded by his enemy, and forced to grind in a prison.[1]

Samson rejected the authority of his parents, and God warns, "The eye that mocketh at his father, and despiseth to obey his mother, the ravens of the valley shall pick it out, and the young eagles shall eat it."[2]

Samson saw a girl that he decided to marry. He told his parents to get her for him. Samson's parents tried to reason with him, but he insisted, "...Get her for me; for she pleaseth me well."[3]

To what spiritual dangers should Samson's father have been alerted earlier in his life?

1. Judges 13-16.
2. Proverbs 30:17.
3. Judges 14:3.

1 BE ALERT TO SPIRITUAL DANGER!

☐ When a wife is more alert to spiritual danger than her husband, she may lose confidence in her husband's leadership.

☐ When a man is not alert to the danger signals that his wife, son, or daughter is rejecting God's basic principles of life, he will experience bitterness, temporal values, and guilt in his family.

☐ When a man is not alert to the symptoms of bitterness, temporal values, and guilt in members of his family, he will allow them to become vulnerable to the destructive influences of wicked men, sensuous women, and Godless philosophies in the world.

☐ God calls all men to "...Be sober, be vigilant; because your adversary the devil, as a roaring lion, walketh about, seeking whom he may devour" (I Peter 5:8).

☐ What does it mean to be alert to spiritual dangers? It means to:
- Recognize false ideas and deceptive reasoning.
- Detect subtle temptations and wrong motives.
- Determine unwise associations and destructive friendships.
- Foresee conflicts and problems before they happen.
- Discern and obey promptings of God's Holy Spirit.

QUESTIONS FOR PERSONAL APPLICATION

> The following questions are amplified throughout this section and specifically answered on pages 32-41.

1 HOW CAN I PROTECT MY FAMILY FROM THE DESTRUCTIVE INFLUENCES OF "HUMANISTIC" PHILOSOPHIES?

2 WHAT CAN I DO TO INCREASE MY SPIRITUAL ALERTNESS?

3 HOW CAN I BE SURE THAT I AM ACCURATE IN DETECTING SPIRITUAL DANGER?

4 HOW CAN I BEGIN TO MAKE MY FAMILY "MIGHTY IN SPIRIT"?

5 HOW CAN I MOTIVATE MY FAMILY TO REMAIN UNDER GOD-GIVEN AUTHORITY?

1 BE ALERT TO SPIRITUAL DANGER!

A. TO WHAT ERRORS IS YOUR WIFE BEING EXPOSED?

Do you know what books and magazines have planted wrong "seed thoughts" in her mind?

Do you know the true spiritual condition of her friends and associates?

Do you know what false ideas are already influencing her thoughts and decisions?

Do you know what sections of Scripture she now needs in order to cleanse her mind of wrong thoughts?

"That was an interesting article, but I still think the husband should be the head of the family."

B. WHAT PHILOSOPHIES ARE INFLUENCING YOUR CHILDREN?

Do your sons and daughters have a clear grasp of basic Scriptural principles?
Do you supervise the education which they are receiving?
Do you know the beliefs of your children's teachers?
Have you interviewed the teachers who are training your sons and daughters?
Do you know what teaching your children should avoid?

"Dad, in order to graduate, I have to take a course on world religions."

C. WHAT QUESTIONS ARE CAUSING DOUBTS IN THE BIBLE?

Do your children look to you as their most important teacher?
Have they asked you questions about life or the Bible that you have not adequately answered?
Are your children sure of their salvation?
Have your children dedicated their lives to the Lord?
Are your children secretly envying the wicked?
Are your children building God's Word into their lives?

"Dad, how could the Bible be accurate if it was passed down by word of mouth for hundreds of years?"

D. IS YOUR WIFE GOING TO OTHERS FOR COUNSEL?

Do you know what kind of spiritual leadership your wife needs from you?
Does your wife ask other people questions about the Bible that she should be asking you?
Does your wife argue with the counsel you give?
Do you think that your wife may have fears and concerns which she has never told you?

Does your wife feel that you are as concerned as you should be about the problems of the family?

"Honey, I was able to talk to the pastor today about our son's problem."

E. DOES YOUR WIFE AGREE WITH YOUR STANDARDS?

Does your family believe your standards are clearly based on the principles of Scripture?
Does your family believe that your standards for them are consistent with what you do?
Do your children sense that you and your wife do not agree on standards and discipline?
Does your family accept the Bible as the inspired Word of God and the final authority for their lives?

"I wonder if we are too strict with our daughter."

CAN YOU DETECT EARLY WARNINGS OF REBELLION?

☐ **AWARENESS OF TENSION BETWEEN PARENTS.**

WHEN A CHILD SENSES CONFLICT between the parents, the child tends to take up an offense against one or both parents and ultimately rejects the authority of both parents.

☐ **ACCUSATIONS THAT PARENTS ARE SHOWING FAVORITISM.**

A CHILD HAS A KEEN SENSE OF FAIRNESS. Once a parent shows unfairness, the child will feel rejected and accuse the parents of favoritism. This will produce seeds of resentment which grow into rebelliousness.

☐ **FEELINGS OF INFERIORITY AND EVIDENCES OF SELF-REJECTION.**

IF A SON OR DAUGHTER REJECTS THE DESIGN of unchangeable physical features, he or she will also tend to reject the Designer and His authority in daily living.

☐ **LOYALTY TO FRIENDS WHO REJECT AUTHORITY.**

WRONG FRIENDS CORRUPT right living. Also, a son or daughter tends to choose friends who will openly do what that son or daughter secretly wants to do.

☐ **LACK OF CLEAR OR SIGNIFICANT ANSWERS TO THEIR PRAYERS.**

A CHILD WHO "GIVES UP HIS OR HER FAITH" is usually only giving up the parents' faith because the child has never experienced any convincing evidence of a living and loving God.

☐ **EVIDENCES OF PERSONAL MORAL IMPURITY.**

A CHILD WHO VIOLATES God's moral laws will experience guilt which, if not dealt with, will produce rebellion to parents, to the Bible, and to God.

☐ **ADMIRATION OF THOSE WHO MOCK AUTHORITY AND ENCOURAGE REBELLION.**

SCRIPTURE WARNS about the devastating influences of teachers who reject God's principles of authority. These teachers will corrupt the obedient spirit of a son or daughter.

☐ **QUESTIONS ABOUT THE ACCURACY OF THE BIBLE.**

WHEN A SON OR DAUGHTER BEGINS TO QUESTION the accuracy of the Bible, the authority of the Bible is also in question.

☐ **LACK OF CONSISTENT INTEREST IN THE BIBLE OR CHRISTIAN ACTIVITIES.**

SATAN'S PROGRAM OF DESTRUCTION begins with separation from the Bible and Christian friends, and then doubts and defeat follow.

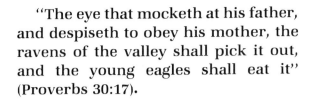

"The eye that mocketh at his father, and despiseth to obey his mother, the ravens of the valley shall pick it out, and the young eagles shall eat it" (Proverbs 30:17).

THE DESTRUCTIVE CONSEQUENCES OF REBELLION

"The eye that mocketh at his father, and despiseth to obey his mother, the ravens of the valley shall pick it out, and the young eagles shall eat it" (Proverbs 30:17). The raven is a scavenger bird. It is usually the first to arrive at the scene of death. It has exceptionally keen eyesight and is able to detect dead or dying prey.

A raven first determines if its prey is dead by picking at the eye of the victim. If the victim does not defend its own eye, it is assumed to be dead. After the raven has begun to satisfy its appetite, the eagles arrive. They are larger and more powerful scavengers, and they finish the work which the ravens began.

These facts from the world of nature add astonishing depth to the warning of Proverbs 30:17. When a son or daughter despises or rejects the authority of his or her parents, he or she begins to show signs of spiritual death. Those evil ones who, like the raven, feed upon destruction, can see the signs of spiritual death in rebellious children by looking into their eyes. "The light of the body is the eye..." (Matthew 6:22).

Paul warned that the one who lives in pleasure is dead while he lives (I Timothy 5:6). Rebellion to authority invites destructive temptation; and after smaller "scavengers" have begun their work, larger ones will come and finish the job.

GOD'S CHAIN OF COMMAND

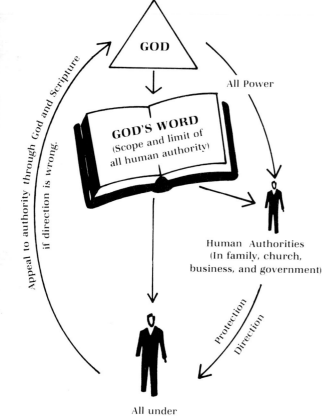

GOD

All Power

Appeal to authority through God and Scripture if direction is wrong.

GOD'S WORD
(Scope and limit of all human authority)

Human Authorities
(In family, church, business, and government)

Protection
Direction

All under authority
(In family, church business, and government)

BASIS OF ANSWERS

QUIZ ON AUTHORITY

1. **My son is usually obedient, but now he refuses to follow my direction on a certain matter. What should I do?**

   a. ☐ Be more forceful in my direction.

   b. ☐ Teach him how to appeal to me through God and the Bible.

   c. ☐ Let my wife take over.

2. **My wife fluctuates from being dominant to being passive toward my direction. What should I do?**

   a. ☐ Give her more freedom to choose her own direction.

   b. ☐ Show her how displeased I am when she becomes dominant.

   c. ☐ Identify our individual responsibilities from the Bible.

3. **My daughter is starting to go around with the wrong kind of fellows. What should I do?**

   a. ☐ Give her more loving protection and direction.

   b. ☐ Have my wife talk to her.

   c. ☐ Tell her that her friends are wrong.

4. **My boss wants me to work a lot of overtime, but I see that it is damaging to my family. What should I do?**

   a. ☐ Tell my boss that I can't work overtime.

   b. ☐ Quit the job and find another one.

   c. ☐ Appeal to my boss on the basis of my Scriptural responsibility at home.

5. **My father thinks that I am being too strict with my children, but I know that some of my present problems came because he was too lenient with me. What should I do?**

   a. ☐ Ask my father to forgive me for the resentment I've had for his lack of discipline.

   b. ☐ Continue to be strict with my children.

   c. ☐ Be more lenient with my children.

BE ALERT TO THE PROMPTINGS OF GOD'S HOLY SPIRIT!

One of the most important aspects of being mighty in Spirit is being able to discern the Spirit of God prompting you to think, speak, and act according to God's Word.

HOW TO RECOGNIZE GOD'S PROMPTINGS

1. THEY ARE INWARD URGINGS TO DO GOD'S WILL

"For it is God which worketh in you both to will and to do of his good pleasure."[1]

"For the grace of God that bringeth salvation hath appeared to all men, teaching us that, denying ungodliness and worldly lusts, we should live soberly, righteously, and godly, in this present world."[2]

2. THEY ARE ONLY UNDERSTOOD BY OUR SPIRIT WHEN IT IS REBORN BY THE SPIRIT OF GOD

"But God hath revealed them unto us by his Spirit: for the Spirit searcheth all things, yea, the deep things of God."[3]

"For what man knoweth the things of a man, save the spirit of man which is in him? Even so the things of God knoweth no man, but the Spirit of God."[4]

"But the natural man receiveth not the things of the Spirit of God: for they are foolishness unto him: neither can he know them, because they are spiritually discerned."[5]

3. THEY ARE IN HARMONY WITH THE TOTAL MESSAGE OF THE BIBLE

"Which things also we speak, not in the words which man's wisdom teacheth, but which the Holy Ghost teacheth; comparing spiritual things with spiritual."[6]

4. THEY ARE OPPOSITE TO THE BASIC DESIRES OF OUR LOWER NATURE

"For the flesh lusteth against the Spirit, and the Spirit against the flesh: and these are contrary the one to the other: so that ye cannot do the things that ye would."[7]

1. Philippians 2:13.
2. Titus 2:11,12.
3. I Corinthians 2:10.
4. I Corinthians 2:11.
5. I Corinthians 2:14.
6. I Corinthians 2:13.
7. Galatians 5:17,18.

GOD IN THREE PERSONS	ILLUSTRATIONS:
1. GOD THE FATHER	1. TRANSMITTER
2. GOD THE SON	2. MESSAGE
3. GOD THE HOLY SPIRIT	3. RECEIVER

GOD GIVES CONTINUAL WARNINGS...

BUT THEY ARE ONLY EFFECTIVE IF WE HEAR THEM.

PROMPTINGS COME BY:

READING THE BIBLE

FERVENT PRAYER

GODLY PREACHING

PARENTS' COUNSEL

WHAT DOES THE HOLY SPIRIT PROMPT US TO DO?

We are prompted to reject evil thoughts.

We are prompted to refrain from gossip and wrong words.

We are prompted to pray for a certain person.

We are prompted to write a letter to a certain person to thank, warn, or encourage him or her.

We are prompted to ask forgiveness of each one we offend in word, action, or attitude.

We are prompted to walk away from wicked people with wrong motives.

We are prompted to give money or possessions to the Lord and to those in need.

We are prompted to spend time reading God's Word.

5. THEY OFTEN FOCUS ON "LITTLE THINGS" WHICH WE THINK ARE UNIMPORTANT

"He that is faithful in that which is least is faithful also in much: and he that is unjust in the least is unjust also in much."[1]

"...The little foxes, that spoil the vines..."[2]

6. THEY BECOME WEAKER AND WEAKER THE LONGER WE RESIST OBEYING THEM

"...Walk not as other Gentiles walk, in the vanity of their mind, having the understanding darkened, being alienated from the life of God through the ignorance that is in them, because of the blindness of their heart: who being past feeling have given themselves over unto lasciviousness, to work all uncleanness with greediness."[3]

"Quench not the Spirit."[4]

7. THEY WARN OF APPROACHING TEMPTATIONS

"Wherefore let him that thinketh he standeth take heed [to the Spirit's promptings] lest he fall."[5]

"Watch and pray, that ye enter not into temptation: the spirit indeed is willing, but the flesh is weak."[6]

"Looking diligently lest any man fail of the grace of God; lest any root of bitterness springing up trouble you, and thereby many be defiled."[7]

8. THEY ARE DEADENED BY MORAL IMPURITY

"Dearly beloved, I beseech you as strangers and pilgrims, abstain from fleshly lusts, which war against the soul."[8]

"Because that, when they knew God, they glorified him not as God, neither were thankful; but became vain in their imaginations, and their foolish heart was darkened...Wherefore God also gave them up to uncleanness through the lusts of their own hearts...."[9]

9. THEY PRODUCE GUILT WHEN VIOLATED

"For if our heart condemn us, God is greater than our heart, and knoweth all things."[10]

"...Their conscience also bearing witness, and their thoughts the meanwhile accusing or else excusing one another."[11]

10. THEY PRODUCE GODLY CHARACTER IF OBEYED

"But the fruit of the Spirit is love, joy, peace, longsuffering, gentleness, goodness, faith, meekness, temperance: against such there is no law."[12]

1. Luke 16:10.
2. Song of Solomon 2:15.
3. Ephesians 4:17-19.
4. I Thessalonians 5:19.
5. I Corinthians 10:12.
6. Matthew 26:41.
7. Hebrews 12:15.
8. I Peter 2:11.
9. Romans 1:21-24.
10. I John 3:20.
11. Romans 2:15.
12. Galatians 5:22,23.

HAVE YOU DAMAGED YOUR FAMILY'S TRUST IN THE AUTHORITY OF THE BIBLE?

HAVE YOU EVER...

☐ Have you ever expressed doubts about the inspiration of the Bible or its accuracy?

☐ Have you ever told jokes which belittled the Bible or its standards?

☐ Have you ever ridiculed Christian leaders for taking the Bible "too literally"?

☐ Have you ever used profanity?

☐ Have you ever said that the Bible is not applicable for the problems of our day?

☐ Have you ever justified a questionable activity by claiming that the Bible can be interpreted several different ways?

☐ Have you ever tried to get direction from horoscopes, **Ouija** boards, fortune tellers, or any other occult practices?

☐ Have you ever told your wife or children to ask somebody else their questions about the Bible because you did not know the answer?

☐ Have you ever gone for long periods of time without reading or memorizing the Bible?

☐ Have you ever brought into your home books or magazines whose primary purpose was to blaspheme the Word of God?

☐ Have you ever formed a close friendship with a man who rejected the inspiration of the Bible?

☐ Have you ever encouraged your wife or children to do things which were contrary to the standards of the Bible?

IF YOU HAVE...
you must confess your wrong to God and to your family. Ask for their forgiveness, and become committed to God's Word.

KING NEBUCHADNEZZAR
He was one of the greatest rulers who ever lived, but he discounted the warnings of God. Because his heart was lifted up with pride, God judged him and made his thinking irrational. When Nebuchadnezzar humbled himself, God healed his mind. He then honored God as "...the king of heaven, all whose works are truth...."[1]

KING SAUL
Saul was probably the tallest man in his kingdom, but his spiritual growth was stunted. He relied on the Word of God until sin gained control of his life, then he tried to get direction by consulting a witch. Because of this, God took his life.[2]

1. Daniel 4:37.
2. I Samuel 28:7.

QUESTION No. 1

How can I protect my family from the destructive influences of "humanism" ?

ANSWER:

There are four ways to protect your family from the destructive influences of "humanistic" philosophies. First, explain what "humanistic" philosophies are. Second, teach your family how to detect them. Third, develop a Godly contempt for them. Fourth, build a "hedge" of prayer around each one in your family.

READ THIS TO YOUR FAMILY

— WHAT IS "SECULAR HUMANISM"? —

"Secular humanism" excludes God. It makes man his own highest authority. It teaches that man's pleasure or happiness is the highest good. Moral standards are relative in humanism and give way to situational ethics.[1]

The philosophy of humanism began with Satan, when he said in his heart, "...I will be like the most High."[2] It was the philosophy which Satan used to trick Eve: "...And ye shall be as gods...."[3] "Humanists" are identified by Paul as those "who changed the truth of God into a lie, and worshipped and served the creature more than the Creator...."[4] Humanism is being promoted in our day through false religions, cults, and Godless philosophies.

Magazines which encourage sexual freedom without the responsibility of marriage are promoting humanism. Advertising which encourages people to live only for the present is built on humanistic philosophy. Government programs which promise to solve social evils without God are humanistic programs.

PROVIDE COPIES FOR YOUR FAMILY.

QUIZ No. 1   CAN YOU DETECT "HUMANISTIC" PHILOSOPHIES?

(Match the laws and Scripture verses by placing the correct number in each box.)

FALSE TEACHINGS OF "HUMANISM"	LAWS WHICH ARE BASED ON "HUMANISM"	GOD'S WISDOM WHICH EXPOSES "HUMANISM"
1. All children are born good. They are only corrupted by outside influences.	☐ A. Laws protecting pornography, sodomy, drug abuse, and other impurity. **Humanistic Reasoning:** It is wrong for the government to legislate morality.	☐ A. "So God created man in his own image, in the image of God created he him; male and female created he them. And God blessed them, and God said unto them, Be fruitful and multiply..." (Genesis 1:27-28). "Lo, children are an heritage of the Lord: and the fruit of the womb is his reward" (Psalm 127:3).
2. All moral standards are relative. People must be free to enjoy whatever will make them feel happy.	☐ B. Laws allowing abortion. **Humanistic Reasoning:** When there is an over-population of any species, it is not wrong to reduce its number.	☐ B. "...By one man [Adam] sin entered into the world, and death by sin; and so death passed upon all men, for that all have sinned" (Romans 5:12). "Foolishness is bound in the heart of a child; but the rod of correction shall drive it far from him" (Proverbs 22:15).
3. The human race has simply evolved from lower forms of animals.	☐ C. Laws prohibiting all spanking. **Humanistic Reasoning:** Spanking children teaches them to become violent.	☐ C. "Knowing this, that the law is not made for a righteous man, but for the lawless and disobedient, for the ungodly and for sinners, for unholy and profane, for murderers of fathers and murderers of mothers, for manslayers, For whoremongers, for them that defile themselves with mankind, for menstealers, for liars, for perjured persons, and if there be any other thing that is contrary to sound doctrine" (I Timothy 1:9-10).

1. Paul Kurtz and Edwin H. Wilson, "Humanist Manifesto II," Current, Ed. Grant S. McClellan, Number 156 (November 1973).
2. Isaiah 14:14.
3. Genesis 3:5.
4. Romans 1:25.

APPLICATION No. 1

1. Purpose to protect your entire family from the destructive influences of philosophies which exalt man and fail to honor Christ.

O God, I pray that You will build a wall of protection around my family. I ask, in the name and through the blood of the Lord Jesus Christ, that You will rebuke Satan in any attempt he would make to deceive me or my family. I claim Your weapons of casting down all reasoning that exalts itself against Your knowledge and bringing into captivity every thought to the obedience of Christ.

---

2. Memorize II Corinthians 10:4-5.

"For the weapons of our warfare are not carnal, but mighty through God to the pulling down of strong holds; casting down imaginations,[1] and every high thing that exalteth itself against the knowledge of God, and bringing into captivity every thought to the obedience of Christ."

---

3. Help your family to identify "secular humanism." Quiz them: "If you were asked to explain 'humanistic philosophy,' what would you say?" (Read the boxed answer on the previous page. Then see if they can match the laws in Scripture with "humanistic" philosophy in quiz.) **ANSWERS: 1. C, B; 2. A, C; 3. B, A.**

4. Give the Scriptural basis for a Godly contempt for man's "wisdom." This could be the Bible reading for one week at the evening meal.

1. ROMANS 1:20-32 "...Professing themselves to be wise, they became fools...."
2. I CORINTHIANS 1:18-31 "...Hath not God made foolish the wisdom of this world...."
3. I CORINTHIANS 2:1-16 "...The natural man receiveth not the things of the Spirit of God: For they are foolishness unto him...."
4. II THESSALONIANS 2:10-12 "...God shall send them strong delusion...."
5. II TIMOTHY 3:1-10 "Ever learning and never able to come to the knowledge of the truth...."
6. II PETER 2:1-3:7 "...They speak great swelling words of vanity...."
7. JUDE 4-20 "...Walking after their own lusts...."

Every wise father will not only build a "hedge" of prayer around his family, but he will instill in the thinking of his family a Godly contempt for secular humanism in all of its forms. If he fails to do this, the humanistic philosophies of our day will teach his family to have an ungodly contempt for him and the authority of the Bible.

1. Imaginations (*logismos*): Philosophical reasonings.

SECOND WEEK:

☐ Study pages 25-27.
☐ Complete Application No. 2.
☐ Identify Quality No. 1 (page 6).

QUESTION No. 2

What can I do to increase my spiritual alertness?

ANSWER:

One of the most effective ways to increase your spiritual alertness is to combine fasting and the memorization of God's Word. This was the very method which the Holy Spirit led the Lord Jesus Christ to use during His wilderness temptation.[1] Jesus promised that if we fast secretly, God will reward us openly.[2]

WHY SHOULD WE FAST?

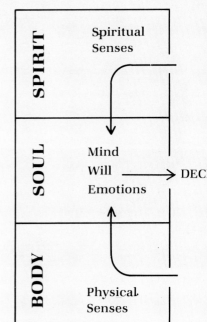

When you eat food, a greater amount of your blood is used for your digestive system. When you exercise, a greater amount of blood is used for your muscles. But when you fast, a greater amount of blood is available for your mental system. When you fast and memorize, you will greatly increase your spiritual alertness and your ability to make wise decisions.

In the same way that we are alert to the physical world through our five physical senses of taste, touch, sight, sound, and smell, we must become alert to the spiritual world through our spiritual senses. Both Christ and Paul were grieved over their followers who had spiritual eyes but could not see and spiritual ears but could not hear.[3]

If you set aside food and beverages (with the exception of water) for one day a week, and spend that day as far as possible in memorizing and reading God's Word, you will be able to look back several years from now and see that God has richly rewarded you with greater creativity, wisdom, fulfillment, physical health, and spiritual alertness. Any progress toward this ideal will be rewarded in proportionate measure.

QUIZ No. 2   WHO DID GOD HONOR WHEN THEY FASTED?[4]

(Match each statement with the correct name.)

1. **This person changed the mind of a powerful king after fasting and praying for three days.**   ☐ A. EZRA

2. **This person was given clear direction for a life work while fasting and praying with church leaders.**   ☐ B. KING OF NINEVAH

3. **This person was given permission and provision to rebuild the walls of God's city after fasting for several days.**   ☐ C. ESTHER

4. **This person was given safety for a dangerous journey after he and his people fasted and prayed.**   ☐ D. NEHEMIAH

5. **This person saved his city from God's destruction because he repented and proclaimed a fast.**   ☐ E. PAUL

---

1. Luke 4:1-14.
2. Matthew 6:16-18.
3. Matthew 13:9-16; Acts 28:27.
4. Jesus promised to reward us openly if we fast secretly. Matthew 6:18.

APPLICATION No. 2

1. Purpose to increase your spiritual alertness by combining memorization with fasting.

> *O Lord, I will esteem the words of your mouth more important than my necessary food.*[1]

2. Set aside your lunch today, and instead, memorize as many of the following verses as you can.

☐ "Moreover when[2] ye fast, be not, as the hypocrites, of a sad countenance: for they disfigure their faces, that they may appear unto men to fast. Verily I say unto you, they have their reward. But thou, when thou fastest, anoint thine head, and wash thy face; that thou appear not unto men to fast, but unto thy Father which is in secret: and thy Father, which seeth in secret, shall reward thee openly" (Matthew 6:16-18).

☐ "Is not this the fast that I have chosen? to loose the bands of wickedness, to undo the heavy burdens, and to let the oppressed go free, and that ye break every yoke?[3] Is it not to deal thy bread [4]to the hungry, and that thou bring the poor that are cast out to thy house? When thou seest the naked,[5] that thou cover him; and that thou hide not thyself from thine own flesh?[6] Then shall thy light break forth as the morning, and thine health shall spring forth speedily: and thy righteousness shall go before thee; the glory of the Lord shall be thy rereward"[7] (Isaiah 58:6-8).

3. This evening, during the mealtime, share with your family the importance of fasting.[8]

☐ You might want to introduce the subject by using a quiz:

"I have a question. Let's see who can give me the right answer. We receive nourishment from our food as we eat it and digest it. We receive nourishment from God's Word as we read it, memorize it, and meditate on it. But there is something that we can do to increase that spiritual nourishment. Do you know what it is?" (Wait for their answers.) The answer is to combine fasting and memorization. (Read material on opposite page. Then give the quiz and reward those who get the right answers.)

ANSWERS:
1.- C (Esther 4:16)
2. - E (Acts 13:2)
3. - D (Nehemiah 1:3)
4. - A (Ezra 8:21-23)
5. - B (Jonah 3:6-10)

1. Personalization of Job 23:12.
2. Note that Jesus did not say IF you fast, but WHEN.
3. Enslaving habit.
4. Physical and spiritual bread.
5. See application to spiritual nakedness. "Clothe them" with salvation (Revelation 3:18, 7:9-17).
6. Flesh and blood (family, relatives).
7. Rereward: Protection from behind; rear guard.
8. A doctor should be consulted on fasting.

THIRD WEEK:

☐ Study pages 8-13.
☐ Complete Application No. 3.
☐ Develop Quality No. 1 (page 6).

QUESTION No. 3

How can I be sure that I am accurate in detecting spiritual danger?

ANSWER:

You can be sure that you are accurate in detecting spiritual danger by being alert to anything that can weaken or violate any basic Scriptural principle or diminish the potential of God's will for our lives.

QUIZ No.3   **CAN YOU IDENTIFY SEVEN BASIC PRINCIPLES?**

Basic Scriptural principles are the teachings of God which are basic to all of life. They are the foundation stones of a successful life, marriage, family, business, and ministry to others. They are the universal prerequisites for true happiness, true freedom, and true fulfillment. [1]

(Can you match each principle with the right definition?)

1. THE PRINCIPLE OF DESIGN:

A. ☐ God has ordained that we discover inner cleansing and joy by learning how to respond to those who offend us. We conquer bitterness by not only forgiving, but by voluntarily investing things of value in the lives of our enemies for Christ's sake.[2]

2. THE PRINCIPLE OF AUTHORITY:

B. ☐ God wants us to dedicate ourselves and everything that we own to Him. He is then able to work supernaturally through us and through that which He entrusts to us. We are then free from the worry and anger which come from claiming our rights.[3]

3. THE PRINCIPLE OF RESPONSIBILITY:

C. ☐ God has promised that if we meditate on His Word day and night, we will be successful in everything we do. To the degree that we are faithful to this principle, we will experience wisdom, understanding, and good success.[4]

4. THE PRINCIPLE OF OWNERSHIP:

D. ☐ Freedom is not the right to do what we want to do, but the power to do what we ought to do. God wants us to experience moral freedom so that we can serve one another in genuine love.[5]

5. THE PRINCIPLE OF SUFFERING:

E. ☐ God made each one of us with His infinite love and creativity. Our unchangeable physical features and family features are designed by God to develop His character in our lives and to build His message through our lives.[6]

6. THE PRINCIPLE OF FREEDOM:

F. ☐ God requires us to be personally responsible for every one of our words, thoughts, actions, attitudes, and motives. If we offend God or others by wrong words, thoughts, actions, attitudes, or motives, we must ask their forgiveness and make restitution.[7]

7. THE PRINCIPLE OF SUCCESS:

G. ☐ God has provided a structure of authority, and He wants each one of us to get under that structure. By being under God's authority, we are protected from the destructive temptations of Satan, and we are given direction from God for our decisions in life.[8]

1. Expanded in the Seminar in Basic Youth Conflicts.
2. I Peter 2:18-24; Matthew 5:44-48.
3. Philippians 2:5-10; 3:7-10.
4. Joshua 1:8; Psalm 1:2,3; 119:97-99; I Timothy 4:15.
5. Romans 6:2-16; I Peter 2:16.
6. Isaiah 45:9,10; Psalm 139:14-17.
7. II Corinthians 10:4,5.
8. Romans 13:1-8; I Peter 2:12-3:8.

APPLICATION No. 3

1. Purpose to make accurate assessments of the spiritual dangers which confront your family.

Lord, I will be vigilant for my family because our adversary, the Devil, as a roaring lion, walketh about seeking whom he may devour.[1]

2. Make a survey of the dangers which threaten your family.

☐ What dangers threaten the self-image of your wife, sons, and daughters?

☐ Defects or scars   ☐ Fashion influences
☐ Inadequacies   ☐ Ridicule by others
☐ Comparison with others   ☐ Guilt

☐ What dangers threaten the obedience of your family?

☐ Wounded spirit   ☐ Influence of television
☐ Wrong friends   ☐ Lack of time with you
☐ Wrong music   ☐ Secular education

☐ What dangers threaten the clear conscience of your family?

☐ Moral impurity   ☐ Unconfessed lies
☐ Stolen items   ☐ Cheating
☐ Fights and arguments   ☐ Broken vows

☐ What dangers threaten the meekness of your family?

☐ Cherished possessions   ☐ Love of money
☐ Cherished friendships   ☐ Rights to style of appearance
☐ Cherished plans   ☐ Rights to music and activities

☐ What dangers threaten the health of your family?

☐ Bitterness for hurts   ☐ Uncleanness
☐ Lack of real forgiveness   ☐ Carelessness
☐ Not going "second mile"   ☐ Wrong foods

☐ What dangers threaten the freedom of your family?

☐ Impure thoughts   ☐ Pornography
☐ Smoking, drinking, drugs   ☐ Television
☐ Sensual habits   ☐ Worldly friends

☐ What dangers threaten the success of your family?

☐ Neglect of Bible reading   ☐ Secular activities on the Lord's Day
☐ No memorization of God's Word   ☐ No experience in fasting and
☐ No meditation on God's Word   studying God's Word
     ☐ No exposure to great Christians

3. Quiz your family on God's principles of life. Offer a special prize.

Answers to Quiz No. 3

1. (E)   3. (F)   5. (A)
2. (G)   4. (B)   6. (D)
     7. (C)

---

1. Personalization of I Peter 5:8.

FOURTH WEEK:

☐ Study pages 14-17, 29-30.
☐ Complete Application No. 4.
☐ Define Quality No. 2 (page 6).

QUESTION No. 4

How can I begin to make my family "mighty in Spirit"?

ANSWER:

You can begin to make your family "mighty in Spirit" by training them to be more alert to the inner promptings of God's Holy Spirit. As you and your family become more alert and obedient to the promptings of God's Spirit, you will experience more of His power and life within your spirit.

WHY DON'T PEOPLE HEAR GOD'S PROMPTINGS?

First, many have never become true Christians through faith in Christ Jesus, and, therefore, the Spirit of God is not in them to give any promptings. [1] They do, however, have a conscience; but this can be easily deadened or distorted. [2] Second, the promptings of God's Spirit are often just opposite to the human reasonings which we have. [3]

QUIZ No. 4   **CAN YOU DISTINGUISH GOD'S PROMPTINGS FROM HUMAN REASONING?**
(Match each prompting with the corresponding human reasoning.)

1. The Holy Spirit prompts me to thank God for the way He made me and for the family He gave me (Psalm 139:14).

   A ☐ My human reasoning is to think that people will respect me more if I never admit that I am wrong or that I have made mistakes.

2. The Holy Spirit prompts me to obey the commands and wishes of those He has placed over me (Ephesians 6:1).

   B ☐ My human reasoning is to resent those who offend me and to hope that they will suffer for what they did.

3. The Holy Spirit prompts me to confess when I am wrong and ask those whom I have hurt to forgive me (Matthew 5:23-24).

   C ☐ My human reasoning is to resent any physical or family deficiencies and - wish that I looked like someone else.

4. The Holy Spirit prompts me to fully forgive those who offend me as Christ forgave me (Ephesians 4:32).

   D ☐ My human reasoning tells me that these things should be done, but that I should wait for a better time to do them.

5. The Holy Spirit prompts me to do things which will benefit the life of one who has hurt me (Matthew 5:44).

   E ☐ My human reasoning is to resent being told what to do and to want to be out from under any authority.

6. The Holy Spirit prompts me to reject impure thoughts and sensual books, magazines, and activities (Galatians 5:17).

   F ☐ My human reasoning urges me to satisfy my curiosity and to at least think about enjoying the pleasures of immorality.

7. The Holy Spirit prompts me to spend time reading, memorizing and meditating on God's Word, or praying for someone (I Timothy 4:15).

   G ☐ My human reasoning is to cut off any contact with one who has hurt me so that I will not be hurt again.

1. Romans 8:9.   3. Proverbs 14:12.
2. Romans 1:21.

APPLICATION No. 4

1. Purpose to train your family to be more alert to the promptings of God's Spirit.

Lord, I pray that you will strengthen us with the power of your Spirit in our inner being.[1]

2. Learn the Scriptural importance of obeying the promptings of God's Spirit. Memorize Romans 8:13.

"For if ye live after the [promptings of the] flesh, ye shall die: but if ye through the [promptings of the] Spirit do mortify the deeds of the body, ye shall live."

3. Ask God to remind you of at least one of the following promptings which He gave you during the past week(s) and which you failed to obey:

☐ A prompting to reject certain impure thoughts.

☐ A prompting to avoid physical danger.

☐ A prompting not to listen to gossip.

☐ A prompting to warn others of danger.

☐ A prompting to show your wife in a special way that you love her.

☐ A prompting to remove a particular item that you know irritates your family.

☐ A prompting to get up early and spend time in God's Word.

☐ A prompting to refrain from turning on the television set in the evening, or to turn it off when an ungodly picture or program is on.

☐ A prompting to refrain from looking at a sensual picture or magazine.

☐ A prompting to tell your family that you were wrong for getting angry, and to ask them to forgive you and pray for you.

☐ A prompting to present the Gospel to someone that you have met.

☐ A prompting to say an encouraging word to someone at home or at work.

☐ A prompting to thank someone for encouraging you.

☐ A prompting to stop and pray for a particular person, and then to let him know that you prayed for him.

☐ A prompting to give a certain amount of money to the Lord or to someone in need.

☐ A prompting not to use a certain word which offends others.

☐ A prompting to fast for one meal or for one day.

4. Obey the prompting which God's Spirit brought to your remembrance (wherever).

5. Explain to your family how God "spanks" you with guilt and "reproofs of life" when you disobey a prompting of His Spirit. (Give an illustration from your own life.)

6. Give your family the quiz on God's promptings: (opposite page)
INTRODUCTION: "Every day we are prompted by the Holy Spirit to do and say certain things which please the Lord, and to stop doing and saying things which displease the Lord. But most people do not hear these promptings because of two major reasons. Do you know what these reasons are?" (Wait for their response, and then read the boxed material on the opposite page. Have them fill in the quiz with the number answers in the appropriate boxes.)

ANSWERS: 1. (C)   3. (A)   5. (G)   7. (D)
          2. (E)   4. (B)   6. (F)

---

1. Personalization of Ephesians 3:16.

FIFTH WEEK:

☐ Study pages 28, and 31.
☐ Complete Application No. 5.
☐ Identify Quality No. 2 (page 6).

QUESTION No. 5

How can I motivate my family to remain under God-given authority?

ANSWER:

There are three ways that you can motivate your family to remain under God-given authority: First, make sure that you are under God's authority; second, explain what happens when anyone gets out from under authority; and third, illustrate this point through appropriate incidents in your own life, or in the lives of others.

WHAT ARE THE CONSEQUENCES OF REBELLION?

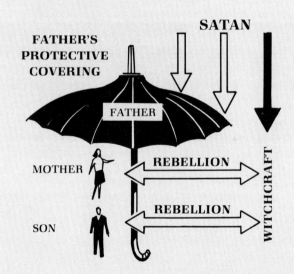

Witchcraft is a devastating sin, but God states that the sin of rebellion is just like the sin of witchcraft (I Samuel 15:23). Both sins take us out from under God's protection and put us under the destructive power of Satan.

God places every person under authority—the authority of parents, government, Godly church leaders, and employers. Every human authority, however, is under the authority of God and the Bible.

As long as we are under God-ordained authority, Satan cannot get through to us with his destructive temptations. If we get out from under the protective covering of our authority, however, we expose ourselves to the realm and the power of Satan's control.

QUIZ No. 5   WHO DID GOD JUDGE FOR REBELLION?

(Match the statement with the correct person.)

1. He tried to justify his rebellion by planning to sacrifice for the Lord.

☐ **A. KORAH**

2. He encouraged rebellion against his father by listening to the grievances of others.

☐ **B. JEROBOAM**

3. He led a rebellion after deciding in his heart that he would be equal with God.

☐ **C. KING SAUL**

4. He promoted a rebellion by accusing his leader of claiming too much authority.

☐ **D. ABSALOM**

5. He organized a rebellion by presenting demands to the new king.

☐ **E. LUCIFER**

(Read illustration on page 27.)

APPLICATION No. 5

1. Purpose to motivate each one in your family to remain under God-given authority.

> *"I pray not that thou shouldest take them out of the world, but that thou shouldest keep them from the evil...Sanctify them through thy truth: thy word is truth."*[1]

2. Think about your past response to authority.

- ☐ Were you obedient to your father and mother?
- ☐ Did you get married with your parents' full approval?
- ☐ Did you have the full approval of your parents-in-law for marriage?
- ☐ Did you ever break the law?
- ☐ Did you ever get fired from a job for resisting authority?
- ☐ Did you ever break a promise or vow that you made to God?
- ☐ Did you ever participate in activities which your parents disapproved of?
- ☐ Did you have friends or music your parents did not like?
- ☐ Did your parents approve of your hair style and dress?
- ☐ Did your pastor feel that you were under his authority?

3. Make sure that you never try to teach from failure, but from corrected failure.

It is very ineffective to try to teach your children from failure. If you say, "Son, don't ever steal, because I stole and I got caught," he will be prompted to say to himself, "Dad, you were not very smart. Now, I can steal and not get caught." A son will tend to want to outdo his father.

The correct way to teach from the past is to teach from corrected failure. "Son, don't ever steal. I stole when I was your age, and it wasn't even important whether I got caught or not. I knew that I was guilty. My conscience wouldn't let me rest until I went back and confessed what I had stolen and made restitution."

4. Take the necessary steps to be able to teach from corrected failure.

- ☐ Ask your parents to forgive you for past disobedience.
- ☐ Ask your parents-in-law to forgive you for marrying against their wishes.
- ☐ Clear your conscience with the civil authorities.
- ☐ Ask forgiveness of any former employer whom you have offended.
- ☐ Ask God to forgive you for broken promises.
- ☐ Ask forgiveness of any pastor whom you have disappointed.

5. Give your family a quiz on authority.

"I have a quiz question. See if you can answer it. The sin of witchcraft is a terrible sin. It puts a person under the direct power of Satan. But God says that there is another sin that is just like witchcraft. What is that sin?" (After they answer, read the material on the opposite page and then share a personal illustration of corrected rebellion from your own life.)

ANSWERS:

1. C (I Samuel 15:22-23)
2. D (II Samuel 15:2-6)
3. E (Isaiah 14:12)
4. A (Numbers 16:1-3)
5. B (I Kings 12:1-19)

1. John 17:15, 17.

WHAT WOULD YOU DO?

If you were required by the government to do something which violated the clear teachings of God's Word, what would you do?

On two different occasions, Daniel was required by the government to do things which violated the obvious teachings of Scripture. His response to the first situation was to explain his convictions to the officer in charge and to respectfully request permission to follow a "creative alternative." [1]

His response to the second situation was to continue obeying God and to submit to the physical consequences of disobeying the king's commandment. [2]

Daniel's Scriptural convictions were used of God to bring him great honor and to accomplish great things for God's people.

1. Daniel 1:8-15.
2. Daniel 6:7-12.

BE TRUE TO GOD'S STANDARDS!

☐   When a man does not know God's principles, he has no basis for discerning spiritual danger.

☐   When a man does not live by God's principles, he sows the seeds of destruction in his own personal life, marriage, family, and business.

☐   A man's standards and convictions must be based upon the principles of life which God has established. These principles are universal and non-optional. No individual, family, business, or nation can violate them without experiencing the conflicts and consequences which will follow.

☐   A wise man will learn these principles and form basic convictions around them. These convictions will give him a strong foundation for personal decisions and also for the training of his own sons and daughters.

☐   What does it mean to be true to God's standards? It means to:

- Know God's basic principles of life.
- Choose to live by God's principles, whatever the cost.
- Translate basic principles into Scriptural convictions.
- Commit yourself to becoming conformed to the character of Christ as a result of following Scriptural convictions.

QUESTIONS FOR PERSONAL APPLICATION

The following questions are amplified throughout this section and specifically answered on pages 48-59.

6 HOW CAN I HELP MY FAMILY TO APPRECIATE THE WISDOM AND ACCURACY OF THE BIBLE?

7 IS THERE A UNIQUE, NON-OFFENSIVE WAY TO LET MY FAMILY REALIZE HOW LITTLE THEY KNOW ABOUT THE BIBLE?

8 WHAT CAN I DO TO HELP MY FAMILY ESTABLISH THE PERSONAL DISCIPLINE OF DAILY BIBLE READING?

9 HOW CAN I HELP MY FAMILY THROUGH THE TIMES WHEN THEY SEEM TO GET NOTHING FROM THE BIBLE?

10 HOW DO I PLAN AN EARLY MORNING OUTING WITH THE BIBLE?

11 HOW CAN I TEACH MY FAMILY TO BE TRUE TO GOD'S STANDARDS IN THEIR OWN LIVES?

BE TRUE TO GOD'S STANDARDS!

CONVICTION No. 1

> **ALL SCRIPTURE IS THE INSPIRED WORD OF GOD AND THE FINAL AUTHORITY FOR MY LIFE.**

WHAT DOES THIS CONVICTION MEAN?

A. **THIS CONVICTION MEANS THAT THE BIBLE IS GOD'S MESSAGE TO MAN, NOT MAN'S MESSAGE ABOUT GOD**

False teachers have consistently tried to prove that the Bible was designed and written only by men. Their purpose in doing this has been to remove the authority of God from its message.

They have pictured the Bible as simply a collection of human writings about God. The fact is that God, not men, initiated the action of writing the Bible.

B. **THIS CONVICTION MEANS THAT EVERY WRITER OF THE BIBLE WROTE WITHOUT ANY ERROR**

Those who seek to discredit the authority of the Bible assume that it contains contradictions and mistakes. They base this theory on their false assumption that the Bible was authored by fallible men rather than by the Holy Spirit. If Scripture contained mistakes, then we would have to depend upon human intellect to determine which parts were accurate and which parts were inaccurate. This would make the intellect of man the final authority in life rather than the eternal Word of God!

C. **THIS CONVICTION MEANS THAT GOD WAS NOT LIMITED BY THE KNOWLEDGE OF THE WRITERS OF THE BIBLE**

Another false assumption in the minds of Bible critics is that the writers of Scripture could not go beyond their own knowledge, cultural background, and experience. This erroneous presumption totally avoids the obvious nature and purpose of the Bible.

God's ways and thoughts are far above our ways and thoughts. He translates His ways and thoughts into our language through the Bible.

Amazing accuracy was achieved by scribes as they diligently made copies of original manuscripts which were "...inspired by the Holy Ghost."[1]

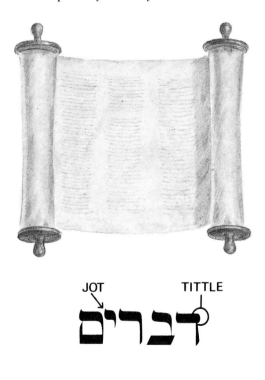

JOT   TITTLE

דברים

"The words of the Lord are pure words: as silver tried in a furnace of earth, purified seven times."[2]

"...Till heaven and earth pass, one jot or one tittle shall in no wise pass from the law, till all be fulfilled."[3]

1. II Peter 1:20, 21.
2. Psalm 12:6.
3. Matthew 5:18.

"I have yet many things to say unto you, but ye cannot bear them now. Howbeit when he, the Spirit of truth, is come, he will guide you into all truth...."[2]

GOD'S SPIRIT

GOD

HUMAN SPIRIT

"For what man knoweth the things of a man, save the spirit of man which is in him? even so the things of God knoweth no man, but [unless] the Spirit of God [be in him]. Now we [as believers] have received, not the spirit of the world, but the spirit which is of God; that we might know the things that are freely given to us of God."[3]

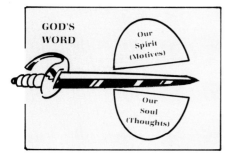

GOD'S WORD

Our Spirit (Motives)

Our Soul (Thoughts)

"For the word of God is quick, and powerful, and sharper than any twoedged sword, piercing even to the dividing asunder of soul and spirit...and is a discerner of the thoughts and intents of the heart."[4]

If God were limited by the knowledge of the writers, the Bible would indeed be a human book with errors and no prophetic accuracy. However, God emphasizes that the writers of Scripture often did not understand the meaning of what they wrote.

D. THIS CONVICTION MEANS THAT THE HOLY SPIRIT TEACHES ME TO UNDERSTAND THE INTERPRETATION OF GOD'S WORD AND ITS APPLICATION TO DAILY LIVING

There is only one interpretation of Scripture. No Scripture is of any private interpretation.[5] However, there are many applications of Scripture. For example, "Thou shalt not steal" has only one interpretation: Do not take what belongs to someone else. But it has many applications: Do not steal money, do not steal time, do not steal affections.

Those who listened to the Lord Jesus Christ teach were astonished at the power and authority by which He spoke.[6] His power came as He interpreted the true meaning of the law and also made practical application to the lives of His listeners.

This is precisely the present teaching ministry of the Holy Spirit in the life of every believer.

E. THIS CONVICTION MEANS THAT MY ABILITY TO UNDERSTAND THE BIBLE IS NOT DETERMINED BY MY INTELLECTUAL SKILLS, BUT BY MY RELATIONSHIP TO THE HOLY SPIRIT

Many believe that by intellectual ability alone, we can arrive at the true meaning of Scripture. This is not true. To the degree that we reject God's moral standards, we are incapable of accurately interpreting the message of the Bible.[7]

God's first requirement for accurate interpretation of the Bible is that we be born-again Christians.[8]

God's second requirement for understanding the Bible is that we remove anything from our lives that would grieve the Holy Spirit and quench His power in us.

F. THIS CONVICTION MEANS THAT THE BIBLE MUST BE MY FINAL AUTHORITY FOR DAILY DECISIONS

The only way that we will be truly successful in life is to obey the basic principles of Scripture. However, these principles are opposite to the desires of our lower nature. It is for this reason that we must saturate our minds with the truths of Scripture.

God's Word will reveal our hidden motives which are contrary to His will; and as we delight ourselves in His Word, He will give us new desires which will be in harmony with His principles.[9]

---

1. I Peter 1:10, 12.
2. John 16:12-13.
3. I Corinthians 2:11-12.
4. Hebrews 4:12.
5. II Peter 1:20.
6. Matthew 7:28-29.
7. Romans 1:21; II Thessalonians 2:11-12.
8. I Corinthians 2:11-14.
9. Psalm 37:4.

G. THIS CONVICTION MEANS THAT THE WORDS OF THE BIBLE ARE LIFE-GIVING EXPRESSIONS OF GOD'S WISDOM AND CHARACTER

Man became a living being when God "...breathed into his nostrils the breath of life...."[1] Similarly, the words of the Bible arc "God-breathed."[2] They produce spiritual life and growth in the life of a believer.

We are commanded by God to be filled with His Spirit[3] and to be filled with His Word.[4] The Word and the Spirit produce God's wisdom and character in our lives. "Whereby are given unto us exceeding great and precious promises: that by these ye might be partakers of the divine nature...."[5]

H. THIS CONVICTION MEANS THAT THE WORDS OF THE BIBLE CAN BE USED TO CONQUER THE POWER OF SATAN

It is not enough to accept the authority of Scripture for ourselves. We must use it to overcome the power of the devil in our own lives and in the lives of those under our spiritual protection.

The Lord Jesus demonstrated how to use the words of Scripture to defeat Satan. Three times He resisted Satan by quoting the precise Scriptures to counter his temptations.[6]

This is one of the most important reasons for committing ourselves to the inspiration and authority of the Bible. We can use it in the spiritual warfare that encircles every Christian.

The only offensive weapon we have against Satan is the Word of God.[7] God commands us to resist the devil and he will flee from us.[8] We resist him in the name and by the blood of the Lord Jesus Christ and by the Word of God.

Satan wants to bind us with sin and then bring destructive temptations to those under our spiritual care. We must learn how to use the Word of God to bind Satan and then rescue those who are taken captive by him.[9]

The Word of God must be used to conquer the power of sin, or Satan will use sin to conquer the spiritual potential of the father and his family. "No man can enter into a strong man's house, and spoil his goods, except he will first bind the strong man; and then he will spoil the house."[9]

"As newborn babes, desire the sincere milk of the word, that ye may grow thereby."[10]

"...The words that I speak unto you, they are spirit, and they are life."[11]

"...Man shall not live by bread alone, but by every word that proceedeth out of the mouth of God."[12]

HELMET (SALVATION)

BREASTPLATE (RIGHTEOUSNESS)

SWORD (GOD'S WORD)

SHIELD (FAITH)

LOIN BAND (TRUTH)

SHOES (PREPARATION OF GOSPEL OF PEACE)

"For we wrestle not against flesh and blood, but against principalities, against powers, against the rulers of the darkness of this world, against spiritual wickedness in high places."[13]

"Wherefore take unto you the whole armor of God, that ye may be able to withstand in the evil day, and having done all, to stand."[14]

Heavenly Father, in the name of the Lord Jesus Christ and through His blood, rebuke Satan for defeating my son or daughter with moral impurity, for Your Word says that "sin shall not have dominion over us."[15]

1. Genesis 2:7.
2. II Timothy 3:16. Inspired: "God-breathed."
3. Ephesians 5:18.
4. Colossians 3:16.
5. II Peter 1:4.
6. Matthew 4:4, 6, 7.
7. Ephesians 6:17.
8. James 4:7.
9. Mark 3:27.
10. I Peter 2:2.
11. John 6:63.
12. Matthew 4:4.
13. Ephesians 6:12.
14. Ephesians 6:13.
15. Romans 6;14.

☐ Complete Application No. 6.
☐ Develop Quality No. 2 (page 6).

QUESTION No. 6

How can I help my family appreciate the wisdom and accuracy of the Bible?

ANSWER:

You can help your family appreciate the wisdom and accuracy of the Bible by showing how practical and precise the Bible is, and by relating the truths of the Bible to the practical needs and questions which your sons and daughters have. You can do this by stating questions which you believe are in their mind or which should be in their mind. But the best way to find out their questions is to ask them privately.

SPECIAL PROJECT: After giving your family the following quiz, ask each one to write out the answer to the following question: "If you could talk to God for five minutes and ask Him any question you wanted, what question would you ask Him?" By collecting their questions, you will be able to help them find God's answers in the Bible.

PROVIDE COPIES FOR YOUR FAMILY.

QUIZ No. 6 CAN YOU FIND GOD'S ANSWERS IN THE BIBLE?

(Match the question with the right verses.)

1.	What can you do to be popular at school?	A. ☐	Deuteronomy 22:5
2.	Should a girl accept a date from a boy who has a bad temper?	B. ☐	Numbers 30:3-5
3.	What should you do if a classmate mocks you for doing what you know God wants you to do?	C. ☐	Proverbs 18:24; 17:17; 19:6; Matthew 5:46-47; John 15:18.
4.	If a girl makes a vow to God and then realizes that it was a foolish vow, what should she do?	D. ☐	Deuteronomy 22:6-7
5.	If a boy is immoral with a girl, what is he responsible to do?	E. ☐	I Peter 3:14; 4:14
6.	Does God want us to learn about false religions?	F. ☐	Deuteronomy 22:8
7.	What does God say about a girl wearing boy's clothes?	G. ☐	Exodus 22:16-17; Psalm 51; I John 1:9
8.	If you hire a man to help you build a roof on your house, and he falls off, does the Bible say that you are responsible for his injury?	H. ☐	Exodus 23:13; Romans 16:17-19; I John 4:1
9.	If you found a bird sitting on a nest, what does the Bible say you can and cannot do?	I. ☐	Proverbs 22:24; 25:28

APPLICATION No. 6

1. Purpose to help your family appreciate the wisdom and accuracy of the Bible.

"Open thou mine eyes, that I may behold wondrous things out of thy law."[1]

2. Study the quiz on the opposite page.

☐ Offer a prize to the one who has the greatest number of right answers.

☐ Give one answer at a time. Then read the related comment. If possible, have someone read the correct verses.

1. **(C)** Learn how to be a friend, and also be prepared for rejection (Proverbs 18:24; 17:17; 19:6; Matthew 5:46-47; John at:18-21).

2. **(I)** An angry person does not know how to yield rights. A true friendship and marriage require the yielding of rights (Proverbs 22:24; 25:28).

3. **(E)** Welcome humility. It allows God to give grace, and grace is the power and desire to live the Christian life (I Peter 3:14; 4:14).

4. **(B)** Tell her father. God demonstrates the protection of being under a father's authority in relating to a girl's vows (Numbers 30:3-5).

5. **(G)** He should follow her father's instructions. God attaches permanent responsibility to a sexual relationship. God's instruction for a girl's immorality also emphasizes a father's authority and "umbrella of protection" (Exodus 22:16-17; Psalm 51; I John 1:9).

6. **(H)** No. Those who learn to spot counterfeit money do it by first becoming totally familiar with good money (Exodus 23:13; Romans 16:17-19; I John 4:1).

7. **(A)** God warns against it. He wants to keep the basic roles and responsibilities distinct (Deuteronomy 22:5).

8. **(F)** Yes. God expects us to take precautions for the safety of others (Deuteronomy 22:8).

9. **(D)** You can take the eggs or the young birds, but not the mother (Deuteronomy 22:6-7). Man creates environmental problems when he upsets the balance in nature. Birds control insects. We kill the birds and use DDT on the insects. Then we find that DDT builds up poison in our food and in our bodies.

3. Introduce the special project. Ask each one to write out the question he or she would ask God. If possible, collect these questions. Discern which ones might be proper to use for family discussion. Ask permission before sharing questions with the family. Realize that each question reflects personal needs.

1. Psalm 119:18.

SEVENTH WEEK:

☐ Complete Application No. 7.
☐ Define Quality No. 3 (page 6).

QUESTION No. 7

Is there a unique, non-offensive way to let my family realize how little they know about the Bible?

ANSWER:

The following Bible "I.Q." test is a humorous, yet effective, way to show your family how little they actually know about the Bible. Many times we think that we know more about the Bible than we really do know, and this quiz will help to illustrate this fact.

Bible I.Q. Test

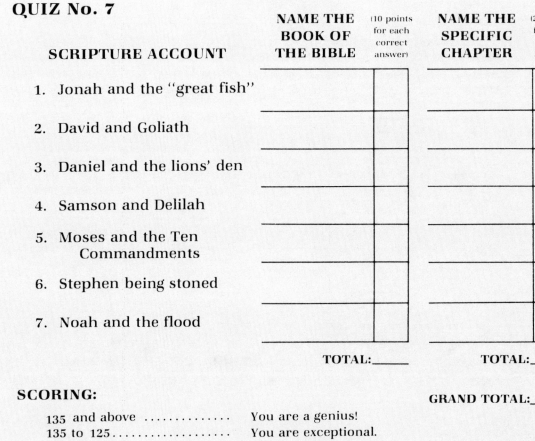

QUIZ No. 7

SCRIPTURE ACCOUNT	NAME THE BOOK OF THE BIBLE	(10 points for each correct answer)	NAME THE SPECIFIC CHAPTER	(20 points for each correct answer)
1. Jonah and the "great fish"				
2. David and Goliath				
3. Daniel and the lions' den				
4. Samson and Delilah				
5. Moses and the Ten Commandments				
6. Stephen being stoned				
7. Noah and the flood				
	TOTAL:_____		TOTAL:_____	

GRAND TOTAL:_____

PROVIDE COPIES FOR YOUR FAMILY.

SCORING:

135 and above	You are a genius!
135 to 125.	You are exceptional.
125 to 115	You are above average.
115 to 105	You are average.
105 to 90.	You are below average.
90 to 75.	You need help!
Below 75.	Bad news!

APPLICATION No. 7

1. Purpose to motivate each one in your family to learn more about the Bible.

Lord, work in my family so that each one of us will desire the sincere milk of Your Word that we may grow spiritually by it.[1]

2. Make sure that each person in your family has a Bible and a pocket New Testament with Psalms and Proverbs.

☐ The Bible should include helpful study notes, especially for the King James language.

☐ Ask your wife to buy a "starter" Bible and Testament for any who do not have them.

☐ A good Bible makes an ideal birthday or graduation gift, but first find out what color and size is preferred.

☐ When you give a Bible, write a personal note and Bible verse in the front page.

☐ An additional New Testament should be a size which can be carried in the pocket or purse.

☐ New Testaments can be excellent prizes for your evening quizzes.

3. Emphasize proper respect and care for the Bible. It is important that children see their parents treat the Bible with respect.

---

4. Begin a mental "practical file" of Scripture passages.

☐ How to grow spiritually - John 15
☐ How to develop genuine love - I Corinthians 13
☐ How to conquer moral impurity - Romans 6-8
☐ How to respond to tests - James 1
☐ How to resist the devil - James 4
☐ How to understand chastening - Hebrews 12
☐ How to reset affections - Colossians 3
☐ How to suffer as a Christian - I Peter
☐ How to gain more patience - Romans 5
☐ How to overcome anger - Philippians 2
☐ How to evaluate love - I John

> Memorize this list of references and ask your wife to quiz you on where topics are in the Bible.

---

5. Give your family the "Bible I.Q. Test."

☐ Read the material in the box on the opposite page.

☐ Make sure that no one is ridiculed for getting a low score.

BIBLE I.Q. ANSWERS:

1. Jonah 1 or 2
2. I Samuel 17
3. Daniel 6

4. Judges 16
5. Exodus 20 or Deuteronomy 5
6. Acts 7

7. Genesis 6, 7, or 8

1. Personalization of I Peter 2:2.

EIGHTH WEEK:

☐ Complete Application No. 8.
☐ Identify Quality No. 3 (page 6).

QUESTION No. 8

What can I do to help my family establish the personal discipline of daily Bible reading?

ANSWER:

Encourage each one in your family to make a vow to spend at least five minutes every day reading the Bible, and then give suggestions on what sections of the Bible to read each day. Before they make such a vow, explain the seriousness of it by reading Ecclesiastes 5:4-6 and Deuteronomy 23:21-22.

QUIZ No. 8   **WHO MADE VOWS TO GOD IN THE BIBLE?**
(Match each vow with the person who made it.)

1. Who "vowed a vow, saying, If God will be with me...then shall the Lord be my God...and...I will surely give the tenth unto thee"?

2. Who said, "I will pay my vows unto the Lord now in the presence of all His people"?

3. Who made a vow after being asked to do so by several other people?

4. Who "vowed a vow, and said, O Lord of hosts, if thou wilt indeed look on [my] affliction...I will give him unto the Lord..."?

5. Who vowed a vow unto the Lord, and said, "If thou shalt without fail deliver [them] into mine hands...I will offer it up for a burnt offering."

A. ☐ HANNAH

B. ☐ PAUL

C. ☐ JEPHTHAH

D. ☐ JACOB

E. ☐ DAVID

CAN YOU ANSWER QUESTIONS ON VOWS?

6. What is the reward of making a vow?

F. ☐ The vow is still in effect. If you vow to read the Bible for five minutes a day and miss a day, ask God to forgive you. Then make up the time (Leviticus 6:5).

7. Why should I limit my vows to what I know I can keep?

G. ☐ We are not to "forswear" ourselves. This does not refer to vows but to the deceptive practice of swearing by an object of lesser importance when you didn't intend to fulfill the vow (Matthew 5:33-37).

8. What if I fail to keep my vow?

H. ☐ Vows are a result of seeking the Lord. God gives wisdom, direction, protection, and success to those who seek Him. "...Pay thy vows unto the most High: and call upon me in the day of trouble: I will deliver thee, and thou shalt glorify me" (Psalm 50:14-15).

9. What if I make a foolish vow?

I. ☐ There are serious consequences for breaking a vow to God. He will "destroy the work of thine hands" and He "will surely require it of thee" (Ecclesiastes 5:4-6; Deuteronomy 23:21-22).

10. Didn't Jesus command us not to make vows?

J. ☐ God will hold a man to his Word, but a girl who is under her father's authority, or a wife who is under her husband's protection can be released from an improper vow (Numbers 30:2-15).

PROVIDE COPIES FOR YOUR FAMILY.

APPLICATION No. 8

1. Purpose to lead each one in your family to the decision of reading the Bible at least five minutes every day.

2. Realize the seriousness of making a vow.

"...The Lord thy God will surely require it of thee...."[1]

"...Better is it that thou shouldest not vow, than that thou shouldest vow and not pay...."[2]

3. Relive the struggles that you have had trying to read your Bible daily.

☐ You tried to get up earlier to read, but it did not work.
☐ You tried to get off by yourself, but your wife felt left out.
☐ You tried to read at work, but there were too many interruptions.
☐ You tried to make new resolutions, but they did not last.
☐ You tried to read when you traveled, but you forgot your Bible, and the television interfered.
☐ You tried to read on Sunday, but your family had other plans.
☐ You tried to read at night, but you were too tired to concentrate.
☐ You tried to make use of some extra time, but you did not know where to read.

4. Remind yourself of the alternatives.

Satan's program is: 1. Isolation (from God's Word).
　　　　　　　　　　　2. Doubts (about God's standards).
　　　　　　　　　　　3. Defeat (for you and your family).

5. In view of your need and Satan's alternative, would you pray right now with your wife and make this vow? (Or reaffirm this vow if you made it in the past but did not keep it.)

"Heavenly Father, I realize that either Your Word will keep me from sin, or sin will keep me from Your Word.[3] Realizing this and also realizing the seriousness of a vow, I do now vow (or reaffirm my vow) to spend at least five minutes every day reading your Word.

6. Ask your wife to assist you in being faithful to the vow that you have just made. Have times when you read alone and times when you read together.

7. Share the vow that you have made with your family.

☐ Ask "How many of you find it difficult to be faithful in reading the Bible daily?"
☐ Tell them that you want to go on record with them that you have made a vow that will solve your struggles to get into the Bible.
☐ Explain that you would be thrilled if any one of them would want to make the same vow, but you would never force them to make it. It must be something that God is leading them to do.
☐ Invite anyone who wants to make this vow to tell you about it.
☐ Meanwhile, encourage everyone to begin reading a chapter of Proverbs every day (the chapter that corresponds to the day of the month), then other sections as God would lead them or as needs and questions arise.

8. Give your family the quiz on vows.

QUIZ ANSWERS:

1. **(D)** JACOB (Genesis 28:20)
2. **(E)** DAVID (Psalm 116:14)
3. **(B)** PAUL (Acts 21:23)
4. **(A)** HANNAH (I Samuel 1:11)
5. **(C)** JEPHTHAH (Judges 11:30,31)
6. **(H)**
7. **(I)**
8. **(F)**
9. **(J)**
10. **(G)**

1. Deuteronomy 23:21-23.
2. Ecclesiastes 5:4-6.
3. Psalm 119:11.

NINTH WEEK:

☐ Complete Application No. 9.
☐ Develop Quality No. 3 (page 6).

QUESTION No. 9

How can I help my family through the times when they seem to get nothing from the Bible?

ANSWER:

"Dry seasons" will come. They are a normal part of growing up spiritually. Teach your family how to respond to them. Ask God to reveal the cause of a "dry season." Realize that there are stages of Bible reading, and anticipate the reward of faithfully reading and memorizing during a prolonged dry period.[1]

QUIZ No. 9

CAN YOU EXPLAIN WHY THERE ARE "DRY SEASONS" IN READING YOUR BIBLE?

(Match each cause with its explanation.)

1. "Cereal" stage

   A. ☐ God's Word is compared to "seeds" in Luke 8:11. The initial growth of a seed is hidden, but in due time it will be seen.

2. Inner Cleansing

   B. ☐ A person who is not a Christian is unable to understand the truths of the Bible. In fact, spiritual truths "are foolishness unto him" because the Holy Spirit who teaches the truths of God is not in his life (I Corinthians 2:14).

3. Hidden Growth

   C. ☐ When a Christian grieves the Holy Spirit by disobedience in his life, he not only loses his ability to enjoy God's Word, but he opens himself up to spiritual darkness and strong delusions (Romans 1:21; II Thessalonians 2:11).

4. Test of Sincerity

   D. ☐ The Word of God is compared to "water" in John 15:3. God uses His Word to sanctify our lives from the discouragement of previous cycles of defeat.

5. "Medicine" Stage

   E. ☐ Sometimes God's Word seems dry, but it is still nourishing[1], and we must esteem the words of His mouth more than our necessary food (Job 23:12).

6. Unconfessed Sin

   F. ☐ If you cry after God's knowledge and lift up your voice for His understanding; if you seek it as silver and search for it as you would for hidden treasures, then you will find the knowledge of God (Proverbs 2:3-5).

7. "Natural Man"

   G. ☐ There are parts of the Bible that we may want to avoid because they are unpleasant, but every word of God is essential for life (Matthew 4:4).

PROVIDE COPIES FOR YOUR FAMILY.

1. Adam Clarke was one of the greatest Bible teachers of the nineteen century. He went through a "dry" period of two years. Each day he faithfully studied the Bible for several hours but seemed to get nothing out of it. Then one day God rewarded him by opening up his spiritual understanding to the great themes, hidden wisdom, and threads of truth in the Bible.

APPLICATION No. 9

1. Purpose to help your family through times when they get nothing out of their Bible reading.

> *"O God, thou art my God; early will I seek thee: my soul thirsteth for thee, my flesh longeth for thee in a dry and thirsty land, where no water is."* [1]

2. Recall the commitment that you made with your wife about wanting God's best—whatever the cost.

☐ The cost now will be one less hour of sleep tomorrow morning.

3. Plan an early morning outing.

☐ Choose a quiet place away from home. If it is warm outside, choose a scenic picnic grove. If it is cold outside, ask your pastor for permission to use a room at the church. (You may need to have your wife get a key from the custodian today.)

☐ Plan to spend an hour there. The precise schedule is given on the following pages. It would be wise to look it over now.

☐ Ask your wife whom you should invite. If she thinks you ought to spend that hour alone, with her, with one of the children, or with the whole family, follow her counsel.

☐ Be careful of promises. If more than the one(s) you ask want to go with you, be very careful not to make promises that you might not be able to keep right now. To a child, the statement, "I'd like to take you, too, sometime," is a promise! He will hold you to it.

☐ Ask your wife if she would pack a little breakfast for you. Also, ask her to check out any other necessary details.

4. During the evening meal, explain what you plan to do.

☐ "As each one of you continues to be faithful in reading the Bible you will experience an occasional 'dry period' when you seem to get nothing out of the Bible."

☐ "We've made plans to do something early tomorrow morning which I hope will encourage every one of you to do on your own as you grow older."

☐ "God will always reward those who make extra sacrifices to spend time with Him and His Word ."

5. Give your family the quiz on "dry seasons."

ANSWERS:

1. **(E)**	3. **(A)**	5. **(G)**	7. **(B)**
2. **(D)**	4. **(F)**	6. **(C)**	

1. Psalm 63:1.

TENTH WEEK:

☐ Complete Application No. 10.
☐ Define Quality No. 4 (page 6).

QUESTION No. 10

How do I plan an early morning outing with the Bible?

ANSWER:

There are two steps to keep in mind when planning an early morning outing with the Bible. First, encourage the ones who are with you to identify with the great Christians of past generations who woke up early to seek the Lord. Second, provide a balanced schedule between spiritual nourishment, physical nourishment, and recreation. Make it a happy time that they will want to repeat.

QUIZ No. 10

CAN YOU IDENTIFY THOSE IN THE BIBLE WHO AROSE EARLY?
(Match each clue with the correct person.)

1. Who got up early to lead his nation in restoring worship to God?

A. ☐ GIDEON

2. Who got up early to set up a sacred monument and make a vow to God?

B. ☐ JOSHUA

3. Who got up early in the morning to check the safety of his brothers?

C. ☐ SAMUEL

4. Who got up early to intercede in prayer for his sons?

D. ☐ MOSES

5. Who got up early to tell all his servants what God had told him in a dream?

E. ☐ ABRAHAM

6. Who got up early to anoint the one in whom God was well pleased?

F. ☐ DAVID

7. Who got up early several times to give God's commands to a stubborn ruler?

G. ☐ ABIMELECH

8. Who got up early to confirm the Lord's call for a particular task?

H. ☐ HEZEKIAH

9. Who got up early to deliver God's rebuke to a disobedient king?

I. ☐ THE APOSTLES

10. Who got up early to obediently begin a difficult journey with three young men?

J. ☐ MARY MAGDALENE

11. Who got up early many times to conquer his enemies in battle?

K. ☐ JACOB

12. Who got up early to tell "all the words" of God's way of life?

L. ☐ JOB

David was a man after God's own heart. He said, "...I myself will awake early" (Psalm 57:8), and "...early will I seek thee..." (Psalm 63:1). God said of wisdom, "I love them that love me; and those that seek me early shall find me" (Proverbs 8:17).

APPLICATION No. 10

1. Purpose to make this early morning outing a very special occasion.*

> "My voice shalt thou hear in the morning, O Lord; in the morning will I direct my prayer unto thee, and will look up."[1]

2. Be sure to set your alarm and get up on time. Bring food, Bible, and softball, football, or frisbee (if outdoors).

3. Provide encouraging and challenging conversation on the way there. Introduce some of the great Christians who got up early to seek God.

4. Explain the schedule when you arrive at the outing.

10 minutes
1. ☐ Begin with prayer. Ask God to open your spiritual eyes to His Word.
2. ☐ Read the chapter of Proverbs for the day. Have each one choose a verse that stands out to him, and after reading, share the verse and why it stands out.

20 minutes
3. ☐ Assign a project and have time alone in the Word. Assign a little more than can be accomplished in the time. Suggest a key chapter related to a known need, or assign the Sermon on the Mount (Matthew 5, 6, 7). Ask each one to memorize at least one verse (Matthew 5:17). At the end of the time, regather for sharing and food.

15 minutes
4. ☐ Quote the memorized verses as you are eating, and share any other insights that you gained while reading.

15 minutes
5. ☐ Enjoy some light recreation.

5. Give the quiz on those who arose early in the morning.

ANSWERS:

1. **(H)** HEZEKIAH (II Chron. 29:20)
2. **(K)** JACOB (Genesis 28:18-22)
3. **(F)** DAVID (I Samuel 17:20)
4. **(L)** JOB (Job 1:5)
5. **(G)** ABIMELECH (Genesis 20:8)
6. **(J)** MARY MAGDALENE (Mark 16:2)
7. **(D)** MOSES (Exodus 8:20; 9:13)
8. **(A)** GIDEON (Judges 6:38)
9. **(C)** SAMUEL (I Samuel 15:12)
10. **(E)** ABRAHAM (Genesis 22:3)
11. **(B)** JOSHUA (Joshua 3:1; 6:12)
12. **(I)** THE APOSTLES (Acts 5:21)

* This outing is designed for you to include one or more members of your family.

1. Psalm 5:3.

QUESTION No. 11

How can I teach my family to be true to God's standards in their own lives?

ANSWER:

After salvation, the first step in training your family to be true to God's standards is to give them an unshakable confidence in the Word of God. Satan's first attack on Adam and Eve was to get them to question the accuracy of the Word of God. The following quiz has been designed to give the basic meanings of inspiration.

INTRODUCTORY QUESTIONS:

☐ Have you ever had doubts in your mind about the accuracy of the Bible? (Discuss.)

☐ Have you ever experienced doubts about the reality of God? (Discuss.)

☐ The quiz tonight will help you recognize the attacks of Satan on God and on His Word.

QUIZ No. 11

CAN YOU RECOGNIZE AND REFUTE SATAN'S ATTACKS ON THE BIBLE?

(Match each attack with the correct statement on inspiration.)

PROVIDE COPIES FOR YOUR FAMILY.

SATAN'S ATTACKS	GOD'S ANSWER:
1. There are some failures in our lives that we just have to live with and accept.	A. ☐ Inspiration means that the Bible is God's message to man, not man's ideas about God.
2. It requires a lot of intellectual ability and training to understand what the Bible is teaching.	B. ☐ Inspiration means that every writer of the original manuscripts wrote without any error.
3. With our advanced learning today, we know things that the writers of the Bible were not aware of.	C. ☐ Inspiration means that God was not limited by the knowledge of the writers of the Bible.
4. We have in the Bible a collection of thoughts about and experiences of the Creator of our universe.	D. ☐ Inspiration means that the Holy Spirit teaches me to understand the Word of God and how to apply it to daily living.
5. Since the Bible is thousands of years old, we cannot expect it to have all the answers to our problems today.	E. ☐ Inspiration means that my ability to understand the Bible is not determined by my mental ability, but my fellowship with the Holy Spirit.
6. There are so many different interpretations of the Bible that we cannot be sure that our interpretation is right.	F. ☐ Inspiration means that the Bible must be my final authority for daily decisions.
7. Since God had to use men to write the Bible, we cannot assume that the Bible is perfect.	G. ☐ Inspiration means that the words of the Bible are living expressions of God's wisdom and character and contain answers for every problem we have today.
8. The Bible is only a helpful resource for the decisions that we must make in life.	H. ☐ Inspiration means that the words of the Bible can be used to conquer the power of Satan.

APPLICATION No. 11

1. Purpose to train your family to be true to God's standards in their own lives.

> *As for me and my house, we will serve You, Lord!* [1] *"I will behave myself wisely in a perfect way...I will walk within my house with a perfect heart."* [2]

2. Exercise your spiritual ability to discern that all Scripture is the inspired Word of God and the final authority for your life.

3. Commit yourself to this conviction. Resolve to live by it and to demonstrate its truth to your wife and family.

4. Study the basic aspects of inspiration (pages 45-47).

5. Recall the doubts and subtle attacks which Satan has brought to your mind over the years regarding the accuracy of the Bible and the motives of God.

☐ "You can't understand the Bible." ☐ "God doesn't want you to have any fun."
☐ "There are errors in the Bible." ☐ "God doesn't want you to use your mind."
☐ "What about all the interpretations?" ☐ "God didn't answer an important prayer."

6. Recall an incident in your life by which God proved His reality to you.

☐ A time when you sensed the nearness of God.
☐ An incident in which God gave you a special correction.
☐ The recognition of God's laws in your mind because of the guilt that you felt when you broke His laws.
☐ An unusual answer to prayer.

7. Share these experiences with your family through the introductory questions on the opposite page.

8. From time to time emphasize this fact to your family: "We could never exhaust the insights or the applications of the Bible! The more we learn, the more there is to learn."

9. One of the most destructive ideas for sons or daughters to have is the idea that they know enough about the Bible. Your job as a father is to keep renewing their desire for, and their delight in, the rich truths of the Bible.

10. Give your family the quiz on Satan's attacks.

ANSWERS:

1. **(H)**   5. **(G)**
2. **(E)**   6. **(D)**
3. **(C)**   7. **(B)**
4. **(A)**   8. **(F)**

---

1. Personalization of Joshua 24:15.

2. Psalm 101:2.

WHAT MADE HIM SUCCESSFUL?

God promised Joshua that he would have "good success" in everything that he did if he would faithfully perform one activity.

God also promises us that whatever we do will prosper if we are only faithful to this one activity.[1] We will be wiser than all of our enemies, have more understanding than all of our teachers, and understand more than the ancients, if we carry on this one activity.[2]

This activity is meditation on God's Word day and night. Joshua was made successful through meditating on Scripture. God commanded him, "This book of the law shall not depart out of thy mouth; but thou shalt meditate therein day and night, that thou mayest observe to do according to all that is written therein: for then thou shalt make thy way prosperous, and then thou shalt have good success."[3]

1. Psalm 1:2-3.
2. Psalm 119:97-110.
3. Joshua 1:8.

BE A MAN!

☐ When a man fails to achieve God's potential for his life, he experiences frustration with himself and boredom with his work.

☐ A man is a man when he applies Scriptural convictions to his own personal life, whatever the cost. He is a man when he is ready to stand alone rather than to compromise his convictions.

☐ What a man is before God is more important than what he is or what he does for God or for others.

☐ How does God want a man to demonstrate that he is a man? By taking steps to:

- Be a man of confidence!
  Quote the Scripture behind God's principles and your convictions.
- Be a man of accuracy!
  Check out key Bible words in the original languages.
- Be a man of wisdom!
  Meditate on God's Word day and night.
- Be a man of understanding!
  Make practical application of God's Word.
- Be a man of discernment!
  Explain human nature on the basis of Scriptural insights.
- Be a man of action!
  Apply God's Word to your own life, whatever the cost.
- Be a man of power!
  Use Scripture to conquer the power of Satan.

QUESTIONS FOR PERSONAL APPLICATION

The following questions are amplified throughout this section and specifically answered on pages 82-107.

12 WHY IS IT SO IMPORTANT FOR ME AND FOR EACH ONE IN MY FAMILY TO LIVE BY THE CONVICTION OF BIBLICAL AUTHORITY?

13 HOW CAN I INSTRUCT MY FAMILY TO REJECT ANY COUNSEL WHICH IS CONTRARY TO THE BIBLE?

14 HOW CAN I BE SURE THAT I HAVE THE CORRECT INTERPRETATION OF A VERSE OF SCRIPTURE?

15 IF I AM RESPONSIBLE FOR THE LEADERSHIP OF MY FAMILY, HOW CAN I ALWAYS BE SURE THAT MY DECISIONS ARE RIGHT?

16 HOW CAN I LEARN TO DELIGHT MYSELF IN THE LORD SO THAT HE WILL GIVE ME THE DESIRES OF MY HEART?

17 HOW CAN I UNDERSTAND WHAT IS REALLY HAPPENING IN THIS COMPLEX WORLD?

18 HOW CAN I TEACH MY FAMILY TO AVOID ARGUMENTS OVER RELIGION AND PHILOSOPHY?

19 HOW CAN I RECOGNIZE THE THINGS IN MY HOME WHICH ARE HINDERING THE POWER OF THE WORD OF GOD?

20 HOW CAN I LEARN TO OVERCOME THE POWER OF TEMPTATIONS IN MY LIFE?

21 HOW CAN A FATHER CONQUER SATAN'S DECEPTIONS WITH PRECISE SCRIPTURE?

3 BE A MAN! BE A MAN OF CONFIDENCE!

BE ABLE TO QUOTE THE SCRIPTURE BEHIND YOUR CONVICTIONS

TEN VERSES EVERY MAN SHOULD MEMORIZE:

A. "All scripture is given by inspiration of God, and is profitable for doctrine, for reproof, for correction, for instruction in righteousness: that the man of God may be perfect, throughly furnished unto all good works" (II Timothy 3:16-17).

B. "Knowing this first, that no prophecy of the scripture is of any private interpretation. For the prophecy came not in old time by the will of man: but holy men of God spake as they were moved by the Holy Ghost" (II Peter 1:20-21).

C. "...Man shall not live by bread alone, but by every word that proceedeth out of the mouth of God" (Matthew 4:4).

D. "...Thou hast magnified thy word above all thy name" (Psalm 138:2).

E. "Every word of God is pure: he is a shield unto them that put their trust in him. Add thou not unto his words, lest he reprove thee, and thou be found a liar" (Proverbs 30:5-6).

F. "The words of the Lord are pure words: as silver tried in a furnace of earth, purified seven times..." (Psalm 12:6). "And it is easier for heaven and earth to pass, than one tittle of the law to fail" (Luke 16:17).

G. "Think not that I am come to destroy the law, or the prophets: I am not come to destroy, but to fulfil. For verily I say unto you, till heaven and earth pass, one jot or one tittle shall in no wise pass from the law, till all be fulfilled" (Matthew 5:17-18).

H. "...When ye received the word of God which ye heard of us, ye received it not as the word of men, but as it is in truth, the word of God, which effectually worketh also in you that believe" (I Thessalonians 2:13).

I. "...[You have been] born again, not of corruptible seed, but of incorruptible, by the word of God, which liveth and abideth forever" (I Peter 1:23).

J. "And for this cause God shall send them strong delusion, that they should believe a lie: that they all might be damned who believed not the truth, but had pleasure in unrighteousness" (II Thessalonians 2:11, 12).

You can be sure that Satan will bring doubts to you, your wife, and your children regarding the authority of God's Word. Can you answer him with Scripture?

HOW TO MEMORIZE A VERSE

1. Read it several times.
2. Look up difficult words.
3. Picture key words.
4. Learn one phrase at a time.
5. Repeat previous phrases as you quote new ones.
6. Quote the verse to the Lord as you go to sleep.
7. Repeat the verse to the Lord as you wake up.

HOW A FATHER CAN BE MOTIVATED TO MEMORIZE SCRIPTURE

1. Set an achievable goal. Resolve to learn one verse a day for ten days.
2. Be accountable to someone. Ask your wife to quiz you each evening before dinner.
3. Attach a reward to it. If you can quote it "word perfect," you can eat.
4. Attach a consequence to it. If you can't quote it, do not eat until you can quote it perfectly.

Suppose you were called before a court of law to determine if your beliefs are based on convictions or on preferences.

You are asked to state your religious convictions and you answer:

"My first conviction is ,that the Bible is the inspired, infallible Word of God and the final authority for my life."

This conviction is vital to everything else you say.

Now, what if they cross-examine you? If they ask you for the Scripture upon which you base your conviction, would you be ready to give it to them?

LET YOUR FAMILY BE A GREATER PART OF YOUR LIFE

Ask you wife, son, or daughter to write out or type out these ten verses on ten 3" x 5" cards. By being able to carry the cards with you, you will be able to memorize the verses more easily.

QUIZ YOURSELF

Ask your wife, son, or daughter to quiz you by asking the following questions and having you quote the right verse—word perfect!

1. **IS THE ENTIRE BIBLE INSPIRED?**

☐ Quote II Timothy 3:16.

2. **HOW DO YOU KNOW THAT THE BIBLE IS FROM GOD?**

☐ Quote II Peter 1:20-21.

3. **WHY IS THE BIBLE SO IMPORTANT TO LIVING?**

☐ Quote Matthew 4:4.

4. **CAN GOD CHANGE HIS WORD TO CHANGING TIMES?**

☐ Quote Psalm 119:160.

5. **IS EVERY WORD IN THE ORIGINAL MANUSCRIPTS ACCURATE?**

☐ Quote Proverbs 30:5-6.

6. **HOW DO YOU KNOW THAT THE BIBLE IS STILL PURE?**

☐ Quote Psalm 12:6; Luke 16:17.

7. **DID CHRIST DO AWAY WITH OLD TESTAMENT LAW?**

☐ Quote Matthew 5:17-18.

8. **DID THE EARLY CHURCH BELIEVE IN INSPIRATION?**

☐ Quote I Thessalonians 2:13.

9. **WHY DO YOU PUT SO MUCH TRUST IN THE BIBLE?**

☐ Quote I Peter 1:23.

10. **WHY DO SOME PEOPLE REJECT INSPIRATION?**

☐ Quote II Thessalonians 2:11-12.

When you ask a son or daughter to quiz you on the verses that you have learned, you illustrate the importance of the Bible to them, and you instill in their minds the truths that you are learning.

BE A MAN OF ACCURACY!

LEARN TO CHECK THE ORIGINAL WORD MEANINGS

THE ORIGINAL LANGUAGES:

The Old Testament: Hebrew
The New Testament: Greek

The New Testament was written in the Greek language during the middle of the *Koine* period. Thus, a copy of the original is often referred to as the *Koine* Greek New Testament.

The Old Testament was also translated into the Greek. This is called the *Septuagint*. Many other Christian writings of the second century A.D. were written in *Koinē* Greek. These writings help in understanding the precise meanings of words used in the New Testament.

In many ways, the Greek language is more precise than the English language. Shades of meaning are often lost in the translation. It is important for every father to learn how to search for the original word meanings of the Old and New Testaments.

BASIC METHOD OF RESEARCH:

> **"...No prophecy of the Scripture is of any private interpretation" (II Peter 1:20).**

- Look up the word "private" in <u>Strong's Exhaustive Concordance of the Bible</u>. (<u>Young's Analytical Concordance to the Bible</u> would serve equally well.)

- Write down the italicized number listed after II Peter 1:20. This number is *2398*.

- Look up the number *2398* in the <u>Greek Dictionary</u> in the back of the concordance. The Greek word "idios" is given along with its precise meanings in English.

- Think through the implications of the precise meanings: "one's own" or "separate."

No Scripture is of anyone's personal interpretation—the original writer's or the present day reader's. The writers of Scripture did not put their own construction upon the words they wrote. This is significant. The writers were not presenting their own opinions, but were writing down God's Word.

BASIC RESEARCH LIBRARY

**ALEXANDER THE GREAT
IN BATTLE**

Because of the conquests of Alexander the Great, Greek became the language of the common people. The Greek word *koine* means "common." *Koine* Greek became the language of the civilized world from about 350 years before Christ to about 500 years after Christ.

STRONG'S CONCORDANCE

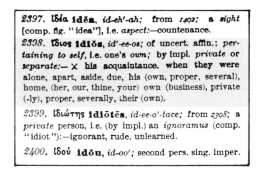

```
prisons
Lu 21:12 up to the synagogues, and into p'.   5438
Ac 22: 4 delivering into p' both men and      "
2Co 11:23 in p' more frequent, in deaths oft. "
private  See also PRIVY.
2Pe 1:20 is of any p' interpretation.         2398
privately  See also PRIVILY.
M't 24: 3 disciples came unto him p'.   2596,2898
M'r 6:32 into a desert place by ship p'.  *  "
     9:28 his disciples asked him p', Why "  "
    13: 3 John and Andrew asked him p'.  "   "
Lu 9:10 aside p' into a desert place    *    "
   10:23 and said p'. Blessed are the eyes" "
Ac 23:19 and went with him aside p', and"    "
Gal 2: 2 but p' to them which were of    "   "
privily  See also PRIVATELY.
```

2397. Ἰδία idéa, id-eh'-ah; from *1492*; a *sight*
[comp. fig. "idea"], i.e. *aspect*:—countenance.
2398. Ἰδιος idios, id'-ee-os; of uncert. affin.; *per-taining to self*, i.e. one's *own*; by impl. *private* or *separate*:— X his acquaintance, when **they were**
alone, apart, aside, due, his (own, proper, several),
home, (her, our, thine, your) own (business), private
(-ly), proper, severally, their (own).
2399. Ἰδιώτης idiōtēs, id-ee-o'-tace; from *2398*; a *private* person, i.e. (by impl.) an *ignoramus* (comp.
"idiot"):—ignorant, rude, unlearned.
2400. Ἰδού idou, id-oo'; second pers. sing. imper.

<u>Greek Dictionary</u> in the back of
<u>Strong's Concordance.</u>

LEARN THE GREEK ALPHABET

The word "alphabet" comes from the first two letters of the Greek alphabet: *Alpha* and *beta.*

In order to use an interlinear New Testament, it will be necessary to recognize the forms of the Greek letters.

SPECIAL NOTES	GREEK NAME	CAPITAL LETTER	SMALL LETTER	ENGLISH EQUIVALENT
	Alpha (ál-fah)	Α	α	a
Gamma has the sound of "g" except when it precedes another *gamma* or *kappa, xi* or *chi;* then it has the English equivalent of "n."	bēta (bay´-tah)	Β	β	b
	gamma (gam´-mah)	Γ	γ	g, n
	delta (del´-tah)	Δ	δ	d
Example: εγχρατειαν = enkrateian	epsilon (ep´-see-lon)	Ε	ε	e
	zēta (dzay´-tah)	Ζ	ς	z
	ēta (ay´-tah)	Η	η	ē
When the symbol "ʿ" is written over the first or second letter of a word, the English equivalent should start with the letter "h."	thēta (thay´-tah)	Θ	ϑ	th
	iota (ee-ó-tah)	Ι	ι	i
	kappa (cap´-pah)	Κ	κ	k
Example: ὑπομονη = hypomonē	lambda (lamb´-dah)	Λ	λ	l
	mu (moo)	Μ	μ	m
	nu (noo)	Ν	ν	n
	xi (ksee)	Ξ	ξ	x
	omikron (om´-e-cron)	Ο	ο	o
	pi (pee)	Π	π	p
Sigma is written "ς" at the end of a word. Elsewhere, it is written "σ."	rhō (hro)	Ρ	ρ	r
	sigma (sig´-mah)	Σ	σ,ς	s
	tau (tow)	Τ	τ	t
	upsilon (ú-pse-lon)	Υ	υ	u
	phi (fee)	Φ	φ	ph
	chi (khee)	Χ	χ	ch
	psi (psee)	Ψ	ψ	ps
	ōmega (o-még-ah)	Ω	ω	ō

EXPANDED METHOD OF RESEARCH

> ## "ALL SCRIPTURE IS GIVEN BY INSPIRATION OF GOD..." (II TIMOTHY 3:16).

WHAT IS THE MEANING OF THE WORD "INSPIRATION"?

An English dictionary may give five different meanings for this word, but it would leave us in doubt as to the meaning which the translators had in mind.

1. Look up II Timothy 3:16 in your <u>Interlinear New Testament.</u>

2. Find the Greek word in the verse which corresponds to the word "inspiration." In this case, you will find three English words used to translate one Greek word: "inspiration of God."

3. Turn the Greek letters into their English equivalents:

θεοπνευστος = "theopneustos"

4. Look up the word "inspiration" in an expository dictionary. You will learn that it comes from two Greek words: "theos" which means "God," and "pneo" which means "to breathe." Thus, the literal meaning of the word is "God-breathed."

DEEPER INSIGHTS

By using the <u>Interlinear New Testament</u>, you may have noticed that the English words "all Scripture is given by inspiration of God" are translated from only three Greek words: *pasa graphē theopneustos.*

Pasa is an adjective which means "all." *Graphē* is a noun which means "Scripture," and *theopneustos* is an adjective which means "God-breathed." There is no verb in this clause other than the linking verb "to be" which must be understood. The literal meaning is, therefore, "all Scripture is God-breathed."

This is important, for it teaches that it is the complete writings of Scripture that are God-breathed. The verse is not referring to the human instruments that He used. The final product is God-breathed, and hence, the very Word of God, true and trustworthy in every detail.

This also assures us that the different books will not contradict one another. Paul's writings will not contradict the writings of Peter or James. Scripture can be interpreted in the light of Scripture.

ίστεως τῆς ἐν Χριστῷ Ἰησοῦ.
faith   –   in   Christ   Jesus.
ραφὴ   θεόπνευστος   καὶ   ὠφέλ
ripture   [is] God-breathed   and   profit
δασκαλίαν,   πρὸς   ἐλεγμόν,   πρ
teaching,   for   reproof,   fo
ωσιν,   πρὸς   παιδείαν   τὴν   ἐν
ction,   for   instruction   –   in

An Interlinear New Testament contains the English words under the Greek text.

INSPIRATION OF GOD
THEOPNEUSTOS (θεόπνευστος), breathe), is used in 2 Tim. 3 : 16, o pired writings. Wycliffe, Tynda ve the rendering " inspired of Go

Expository Dictionary of New Testament Words

This is a compilation of the research of many Greek scholars. They studied the Koine Greek New Testament and other early church writings in order to discover how the words were understood by the people who first read them.

> ## BASIC HINDRANCES TO EFFECTIVE RESEARCH
>
> **1. PRIDE** - "...Knowledge puffeth up, but [love] edifieth."[1]
>
> **2. MORAL IMPURITY** "And for this cause God shall send them strong delusion, that they should believe a lie."[2]

1. I Corinthians 8:1.
2. II Thessalonians 2:11.

...As you wake up.   ...As you go to work.

...As you relax.   ...As you sleep.

If you meditate on the verses that you memorize as you go to sleep, as you wake up, as you go to work, and when you relax, you will be wise and successful in everything that you do![1]

> "But his delight is in the law of the Lord; and in his law doth he meditate day and night."[2]

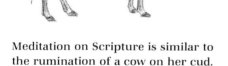

Meditation on Scripture is similar to the rumination of a cow on her cud.

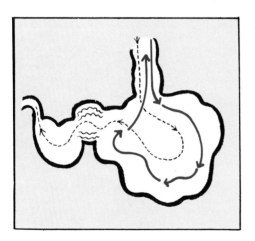

The digestive system of a cow provides a significant parallel to how the Word of God becomes a living part of our being.

1. Deuteronomy 6:7; Psalm 63:5, 6.
2. Psalm 1:2.

BE A MAN OF WISDOM!

MEDITATE ON THE SCRIPTURES DAY AND NIGHT

You can speak with confidence by basing your convictions on the Word of God. You can speak with greater accuracy by researching the precise shades of word meanings. Now, based on these, you can speak with wisdom by meditating on the words of Scripture day and night.

WHY MEDITATION IS SO IMPORTANT

The words of Scripture are living words. They are inexhaustible! They are eternal wisdom within the shell of human words. God wants us to "break open" these human words and begin to discover the rich wealth of personal application and understanding which are in them. This is done by meditation with the teaching ministry of the Holy Spirit in us.

WHAT IS MEDITATION?

● Meditation is a pleasant "murmuring" of Scripture to yourself.
Psalm 1:2: "...In his law doth he meditate...."
Hagah: to murmur (in pleasure), to ponder.

● Meditation is a quiet reflection upon the words of Scripture.
Psalm 119:99: "...Thy testimonies are my **meditation**."
Siychah: reflection with deep devotion; to contemplate; thoughtful utterances of Scripture.

● Meditation is a musical repetition of God's Word.
Psalm 19:14: "Let the words of my mouth and the **meditation** of my heart...."
Higgayown: a musical notation; a murmuring sound.

● Meditation is a prayerful reviewing of Scripture.
I Timothy 4:15: "**Meditate** upon these things...."
Meletaō: to carefully revolve in the mind; to muse upon.

● Meditation is a communing with God in the language of His own written Word.
Psalm 119:48: "...Thy commandments, which I have loved; and I will **meditate** in thy statutes."
Meditation is "talking to the King in the King's own words."

● Meditation is building your day and night around Scripture.
Psalm 119:97: "O how love I thy law! It is my **meditation** all the day."
Job 23:12: "...I have esteemed the words of his mouth more than my necessary food."

● Meditation is worshipping God in spirit and in truth.
John 4:24: "God is a Spirit: and they that worship him must worship him in spirit and in truth."
Psalm 104:34: "My **meditation** of him shall be sweet...."

LEARN HOW TO MEDITATE

1. MEMORIZE A SECTION OF SCRIPTURE.

> EXAMPLE
>
> "MAN SHALL NOT LIVE BY BREAD ALONE, BUT BY EVERY WORD THAT PROCEEDETH OUT OF THE MOUTH OF GOD."[1]

2. QUOTE THE VERSE TO THE LORD AS A PERSONAL PRAYER.

> EXAMPLE
>
> "O Lord, I shall not live by bread alone, but by every word that proceedeth out of your mouth!"

3. REPEAT THE VERSE SEVERAL TIMES. EACH TIME, EMPHASIZE A DIFFERENT WORD.

> EXAMPLE
>
> "**MAN** shall not live by bread alone...."
>
> "Man **SHALL NOT** live by bread alone...."
>
> "Man shall not **LIVE** by bread alone...."

4. VISUALIZE THE SIGNIFICANCE OF EACH WORD AS FAR AS YOU CAN.

> EXAMPLE
>
> "**MAN**..." Every man; all mankind. This is a universal principle. Everyone is included.
>
> "Man **SHALL NOT**...." A final decree. No one will change it. A firm negative.
>
> "Man shall not **LIVE**...." Living is more than just existing. There is physical life and spiritual life. God made us to enjoy the pleasures of life in His presence. Christ came to give us eternal life and abundant physical life. God is life. He made life. He alone fully knows what it consists of.

5. REPEAT THE VERSE. PONDER ON THE FULL MEANING OF EACH WORD.

> EXAMPLE
>
> "MAN, SHALL NOT, LIVE, BY BREAD ALONE, BUT BY EVERY, WORD, THAT PROCEEDETH OUT, OF THE MOUTH, OF GOD."

1. Matthew 4:4.

A Christian family avoided jail and the loss of their Bible by hiding it in a pie!

We read of the martyrs in Church history who had their Bibles destroyed. We think that this cannot happen in our country, but, in effect, it happens every day!

Our Bible is "taken from us" when we turn the lights out to go to sleep. Then, we can only meditate on what we have memorized.

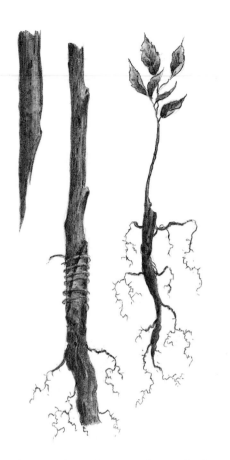

Just as branches can be grafted into a tree and bear new fruit, so we can "graft" God's Word into our heart and produce spiritual fruit.

"Wherefore lay apart all filthiness and superfluity of naughtiness, and receive with meekness the engrafted word, which is able to save your souls."[1]

```
Whatever you ask _____ 19____
PAY TO THE
ORDER OF
_____
and it will be done unto you
on conditions of John 15:7.    God's Word
```

GOD'S "BLANK CHECK"

"If ye abide in me, and my words abide [live] in you, ye shall ask what ye will, and it shall be done unto you. Herein is my Father glorified, that ye bear much fruit; so shall ye be my disciples."[2]

1. James 1:21.
2. John 15:7, 8.

6. REST. LET THE WORDS GROW IN YOUR MIND, WILL, AND EMOTIONS.

This verse is now "engrafted" into your mind. It will grow and bring forth Godly wisdom and character as you continue to nourish it by further meditation.

7. USE THE VERSE TO TALK WITH GOD. PONDER EACH WORD FOR PERSONAL APPLICATION.

EXAMPLE

"Man shall not **LIVE....**" "O Lord, You want me to discover Your life. It is far richer and fuller than I can comprehend. You want to live Your life through me! You want to see through my eyes, speak through my mouth, love through my heart, and work through my hands."

"...By bread **ALONE....**" "If I want Your kind of life, I must concentrate on more than physical food. Food is important, but there is something even more important."

"...But by every **WORD....**" "Lord, every word?...Every word! Every part of Scripture. 'All Scripture is... profitable....' What a task is yet before me! Physical health requires a balanced diet. Spiritual health must require the same. I must learn to gain nourishment from every part of Your Word. If I eat only potatoes day after day, I will tire of potatoes. I would become deficient in other vitamins. If I fail to get a balanced diet from Your Word, I tire of it and become spiritually weak."

8. EXPECT GOD TO BRING THIS VERSE TO YOUR MIND FOR DECISIONS AND SHOW YOU NEW INSIGHTS FROM IT.

EXAMPLE

When you feel spiritually defeated:
"Man shall not live by bread alone...." When is the last time you had a good spiritual meal?"

When you have an important decision to make:
"Man shall not live by bread alone...." Why don't you set aside a day for fasting and the Word?"

When you have experienced a heartache:
"Man shall not live by bread alone...." There are rich insights in the Bible that you will now understand because of this experience.

9. FOLLOW THIS SAME PROCEDURE WITH PSALM 1

BE A MAN OF UNDERSTANDING!

LEARN THE REAL SIGNIFICANCE BEHIND WORLD EVENTS

It is important that a father be able to interpret past and present world events in the light of Bible prophecy, and then live a life that is consistent with the urgency of that message.

REPLACE INSECURITY WITH UNDERSTANDING

A father need not be a history major to understand the facts on the following pages and use them to explain God's news behind current news. If children know what God's program is, it helps to eliminate discouragement and fear about the future.

1. SATAN - GOD'S ETERNAL ENEMY

A. THE PERSON OF SATAN

Your children should be taught that Satan is a real person, just as the Spirit of God is a real person. Satan was created by God. He was a beautiful creature called Lucifer (*hēylēl* - shining brightness). But his heart was lifted up in pride. He desired to be equal with God. Thus, God cast him out of heaven, along with a throng of angels who had followed Satan.[1]

B. THE PROGRAM OF SATAN

Satan fell because he wanted to be his own boss. He wanted equality with God, with no structure of authority over him. This is the essence of rebellion: reserving to myself the right to make final decisions. This is the temptation that Satan introduced to Eve, and Adam, and to everyone after them. All sin can be traced to rebellion. "For rebellion is as the sin of witchcraft...."[2]

C. THE DESTRUCTION OF SATAN

Satan's power was conquered by the life, death, and resurrection of the Lord Jesus Christ. However, he continues to operate in the world. His spirit "...now worketh in the children of disobedience."[3] But he knows that his days are numbered, and that he will be eternally judged in hell, together with all those who reject God's salvation.[4]

1. Isaiah 14:12-16.
2. I Samuel 15:23.
3. Ephesians 2:2.
4. Revelation 20:10.

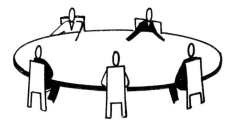

Table conversations are a wonderful opportunity for instilling in children a sense of God's purpose in history and a set of values to go along with it. Martin Luther accomplished much of his childrens' education during his famous "table talks."

SATAN'S PROGRAM

Satan is a deceiver. He hides behind many masks. He counterfeits and imitates. He even transforms himself into an angel of light.[1] The fact that he is now allowing himself to be worshipped openly in this country reveals that multitudes have already been deceived by him and have fallen under his power.

Satan exploits the basic desires of our fallen nature: primarily, the desire to be out from under any authority. He wants us to focus on our rights rather than on our God-given responsibilities.

He appeals to our desire to be our own boss and to live life without any external restraints. He would have us believe that man is getting better and better, and that utopia is every man doing that which is right in his own eyes.[2]

In reality, however, man has always been totally corrupt. The alternative to submission is not freedom but exploitation.

1. II Corinthians 11:14.
2. Judges 21:25.

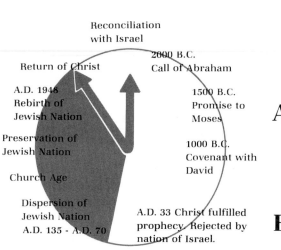

Reconciliation
with Israel

Return of Christ

A.D. 1948
Rebirth of
Jewish Nation

Preservation of
Jewish Nation

Church Age

Dispersion of
Jewish Nation
A.D. 135 - A.D. 70

2000 B.C.
Call of Abraham

1500 B.C.
Promise to
Moses

1000 B.C.
Covenant with
David

A.D. 33 Christ fulfilled
prophecy. Rejected by
nation of Israel.

World events find their true meaning in relation to God's dealings with Israel.

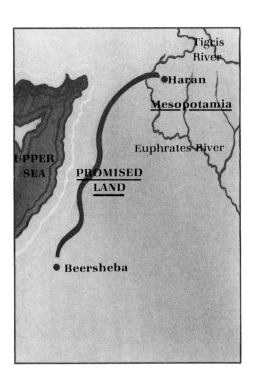

When God called Abram, He promised: "And I will make of thee a great nation...and I will bless them that bless thee, and curse him that curseth thee: and in thee shall all families of the earth be blessed."[1]

In A.D. 70 and again in A.D.135, Roman armies conquered the Jewish people and scattered them to the far corners of the world. For almost nineteen hundred years, they have been away from their land!

2. ISRAEL—GOD'S "TIMECLOCK" FOR THE CHURCH

The key to understanding world events is not in knowing what has taken place in Europe, Russia, or the United States, but in Israel! Palestine is the center of God's arena. That is where Jesus Christ has and will carry out His program. History, after all, is "His Story"!

A. THE "CLOCK" BEGINS WITH ABRAHAM

Approximately two thousand years before Christ, God told Abraham to leave his pagan culture and travel to what is now Palestine. God promised Abraham that He would make of him a great nation.[1]

B. GOD'S PROGRAM CONFIRMED THROUGH MOSES AND DAVID

As an infant nation, there was need for training and discipline. Israel learned the lessons of a servant while in Egypt for four hundred years. Then God raised up Moses to lead the nation back to the land of promise.[2]

Five hundred years later, God clarified His program of redemption in His covenant with David.[3]

C. CHRIST COMES "IN THE FULLNESS OF TIME" AND IS REJECTED

The long-awaited Messiah came to the nation of Israel, but the nation officially rejected him.[4] As a result, the message of salvation was opened up to the Gentiles, and the Church Age began.[5]

D. THE NATION OF ISRAEL IS SCATTERED

Seventy years after the birth of Christ, Roman armies broke through Jewish defenses. The Jews were uprooted from their land and scattered to the farthest corners of the earth. A final remnant of Jews was conquered and dispersed by the Romans in A.D. 135.

The dispersion of the Jewish people for their unbelief was a recurring warning in Old Testament Scriptures. In the very founding of the nation, God assured His people that if they would not listen to Him and obey His Word, "...I will scatter you among the heathen, and will draw out a sword after you: and your land shall be desolate, and your cities waste."[6]

E. THE MARVEL OF ISRAEL'S CONTINUING IDENTITY

For almost nineteen hundred years, the dispersed Jewish people wandered throughout the world. They have undergone astonishing persecutions, but they have endured as a people!

Social scientists, historians, and many "theologians" cannot explain why the Jew was neither assimilated into other nations nor annihilated. The enlightened Christian knows the answer. God is preserving His people for history's final events.

1. Genesis 12:2, 3.
2. The Book of Exodus.
3. II Samuel 7:12-17.

4. John 1:11.
5. Acts 28:28.
6. Leviticus 26:33.

F. THE WORLD-WIDE JEWISH PERSECUTIONS

"And the Lord shall scatter thee among all people, from the one end of the earth even unto the other; and there thou shalt serve other gods, which neither thou nor thy fathers have known, even wood and stone. And among these nations shalt thou find no ease, neither shall the sole of thy foot have rest: but the Lord shall give thee a trembling heart, and failing of eyes, and sorrow of mind:

"And thy life shall hang in doubt before thee; and thou shalt fear day and night, and shalt have none assurance of thy life."[1]

G. THE RESTORATION OF THE NATION OF ISRAEL

Repeatedly in Scripture, God has promised that He would return the Jews to their own land. "And it shall come to pass, when all these things are come upon thee, the blessing and the curse...that then the Lord thy God will turn thy captivity, and have compassion upon thee, and will return and gather thee from all the nations, whither the Lord thy God hath scattered thee."[2]

From the perspective of Bible prophecy, the most significant result of the first and second world wars was to prepare the Jews, and the world, for the restoration of the nation of Israel. However, the full restoration of the nation and its reconciliation to God is yet to come.

H. THE EVENTS OF THE "FINAL ACT" OF HISTORY

The Book of Revelation is illustrated by the picture of marriage. Israel is Jehovah's unfaithful wife and the Church is the Bride of Christ. This is significant, because it throws light on coming world events as they relate to the Jewish wedding ceremony.[3]

JEWISH WEDDING	WORLD EVENTS
1. Bridegroom comes from his father's house to claim his bride.	The return of Christ for His Bride—the Church.[4]
2. Bridal party returns to the father's house.	The rapture of all believers to heaven.[5]
3. Wedding feast for seven days during which the bride is veiled.	The seven year period of anti-Christ and the Great Tribulation.[6]
4. Presentation of the bride to the wedding party.	The second coming of Christ with His Bride and the beginning of His 1000 year reign in Jerusalem.[7]
5. Union that is not to be put asunder.	The final loosing and judgment of Satan, and the eternal rule of God and Christ.[8]

Wide World Photos

The First World War prepared the land of Israel for the return of the Jews. The stirring of "dry bones"[9] had already begun with the first Zionist congress in 1897.

Wide World Photos

The Second World War and Hitler's persecution of Jews prepared the Jewish people for the land of Israel.

Wide World Photos

On May 14, 1948, at 4:30 p.m., the United Nations voted to partition Palestine as a separate Jewish state. Israel was reborn! This signaled the beginning of God's culmination of world history.

Wide World Photos

God's promise of the return of His people to the land of Palestine is now being fulfilled. Since 1948, three million, seven hundred seventy thousand, three hundred Jews have returned to Israel!

1. Deuteronomy 28:64-66.
2. Deuteronomy 30:1-3.
3. Jewish Encyclopedia.
4. John 14:2-3.
5. I Thessalonians 4:13-18.
6. Revelation 4-19.
7. Revelation 20:4.
8. Revelation 20:7-15.
9. Ezekiel 37:1-14

SEE GOD'S NEWS BEHIND THE NEWS

When a nation permits sodomy to become an "acceptable lifestyle," that nation is in its final stages of moral corruption and destruction. "Homosexuality" is not a class of people; it is a type of sin. It results from the Godless philosophy of sex without accompanying responsibility.

Regardless of the political or economic implications of the Mideast, we must always remember God's promise to Abraham: "...I will bless them that bless thee, and curse him that curseth thee..." (Genesis 12:3).

Gold - Nebuchadnezzar (Daniel 2:38)

Silver - The Kings of Media and Persia (Daniel 8:20)

Brass - The King of Grecia (Daniel 8:21)

Iron

Iron and Clay

Daniel 2:37-45

1. INCREASING MORAL BREAKDOWN AND RELIGIOUS APOSTASY REQUIRING CHRISTIANS TO BE MORE ALERT AND DEDICATED

"This know also, that in the last days perilous times shall come. For men shall be lovers of their own selves, covetous, boasters, proud, blasphemers, disobedient to parents, unthankful, unholy, without natural affection, trucebreakers, false accusers, incontinent, fierce, despisers of those that are good, traitors, heady, highminded, lovers of pleasures more than lovers of God; having a form of godliness, but denying the power thereof: from such turn away."[1]

2. EMERGING CULTS AND NATIONAL CRISES

"...Take heed that no man deceive you. For many shall come in my name, saying, I am Christ; and shall deceive many. And ye shall hear of wars and rumors of wars: see that ye be not troubled: for all these things must come to pass, but the end is not yet.

"For nation shall rise against nation, and kingdom against kingdom: and there shall be famines, and pestilences, and earthquakes, in divers places...And because iniquity shall abound, the love of many shall wax cold."[2]

3. CONTINUING TENSIONS IN THE MIDEAST

Palestine will continue to be a focal point of world tension, right up to the Battle of Armageddon, when the superpower from the north and the other nations will fight against it.

"Behold, I will make Jerusalem a cup of trembling unto all the people round about..."[3]

"...And when the thousand years are expired, Satan shall be loosed out of his prison, And shall go out to deceive the nations...."[4] The nations that fight against Jerusalem will be destroyed. Satan will be cast into the lake of fire. God's great white throne will be set up and the final judgment will take place.

4. GROWING PREPARATIONS FOR A WORLD RULER

The expanding world population, the ease of world travel, the perfecting of a world-wide television and communication system, the phenomenal ability of information storage and instant retrieval on computers are only a few of the awesome conditions into which a world leader could suddenly emerge. That leader will be the Antichrist.

1. II Timothy 3:1-5.
2. Matthew 24:4-12.
3. Zechariah 12:2.
4. Revelation 20:7-8.

BE A MAN OF ACTION!

CLEANSE YOUR LIFE OF INFLUENCES WHICH DETRACT FROM GOD'S WORD

1. USE THE WORD OF GOD TO CLEANSE YOUR MIND OF UNSCRIPTURAL IDEAS

Satan knows your weaknesses and your unspoken desires. Based on these, he plants suggestions in your mind. These suggestions are contrary to Scripture, and if acted upon, will cause you to sin. "...Every man is tempted, when he is drawn away of his own lust, and enticed."[1]

All of these thoughts must be cleansed by the Word of God and every new thought and imagination must be brought into captivity to the obedience of Christ.[2]

> **A wise practice for every man to follow is to read a chapter of Proverbs in the morning. Read the chapter that corresponds to the day of the month (i.e., 5th - chapter 5).**

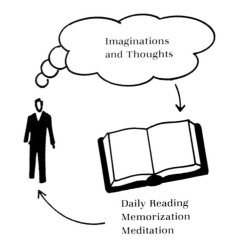

Imaginations and Thoughts

Daily Reading
Memorization
Meditation

"Now ye are clean through the word which I have spoken unto you."[6]

"Casting down imaginations, and every high thing that exalteth itself against the knowledge of God, and bringing into captivity every thought to the obedience of Christ."[7]

2. CLEANSE YOUR HOME OF BOOKS AND MAGAZINES WHICH ARE OPPOSED TO THE BIBLE

At this point it is important to focus on your books only, not those which belong to others in your family. Also, we are not referring to every book or magazine written by a non-Christian, but those which challenge or contradict the principles of the Bible, even if those claim to be Christian.

> **BOOKS TO SEARCH OUT AND DESTROY:**
> **Any religious book written by a false teacher, especially books by cults and false religions.**
> **Any book or magazine connected with the occult, including astrology and witchcraft.**
> **Any book, novel, or magazine which is sensual.**
> **Any book which majors on the humanistic philosophy of evolution.**

It is better to have a few books that honor the Word of God, than a library full of books that challenge the authority of the Bible.

You can expect your wife and children to be attracted to the wrong books in your library!

3. SEVER YOUR RELATIONSHIPS WITH ANY CLOSE FRIENDS WHO REJECT THE BIBLE

God warns us that the wrong kind of friends will corrupt the right kind of living.[3] We are commanded to "...follow righteousness, faith, charity, peace, with them that call on the Lord out of a pure heart."[4]

> **Ask your wife, sons, and daughters which of your close friends are a good influence on you and on them, and which close friends are not a good influence. As you pray for them, and witness to them, the wrong friends will leave you.[5]**

6 TYPES OF "CHRISTIANS" YOU ARE TO AVOID[8]		
FORNICATOR (Perverted)	COVETOUS (Greedy)	DRUNKARD (Undisciplined)
RAILER (Abusive)	IDOLATOR (Heretical)	EXTORTIONER (Dishonest)

1. James 1:14.
2. II Corinthians 10:4-5.
3. I Corinthians 15:33.
4. II Timothy 2:22.
5. Luke 6:22.
6. John 15:3.
7. II Corinthians 10:5.
8. I Corinthians 5:11.

The value system of the father will be picked up by his son. The son may express it in a different outward form, but inwardly he will either focus on that which is temporal (things that are seen) or that which is eternal (things which are not seen).[1]

4. CLEANSE YOUR JOB OF ANY WORK THAT VIOLATES SCRIPTURE

"Treasures of wickedness profit nothing...."[2] Money wrongly gained carries with it a curse.[3] It is better to have little with a clear conscience than great treasures without a right to them.[4]

QUESTIONS TO ASK YOURSELF ABOUT YOUR JOB:

1. Are you making money on a product that damages the lives, morals, or health of those who use it?
2. Are you required to be dishonest or deceptive in any way, or to compromise your convictions?
3. Has God ever convicted you about changing your job?
4. Are the demands of your job forcing you to sacrifice time with God and your family for prolonged periods of time?

---

5. CLEANSE YOUR LIFE OF UNNECESSARY DISTRACTIONS BY READING, STUDYING, MEMORIZING, AND MEDITATING ON THE BIBLE

IF YOU WONDER WHAT YOUR DISTRACTIONS ARE, ASK YOUR WIFE OR CHILDREN

1. What unfinished project is your wife waiting for?
2. What hobbies are cluttering your basement, garage, or back yard?
3. Do you control television or does it control you?
4. Do you have pets that require more time than you give God?
5. Are the magazines you subscribe to taking more time than they should?
6. Is your music honoring to God?

---

6. REPLACE WHAT YOU REMOVE WITH GODLY INFLUENCES IN YOUR LIFE AND HOME

It is not enough to remove wrong influences. To be a man of action, you must also put the right influences into your life and home. Work with your wife on the following items:

---

1. Purchase classic Christian books and biographies and read them.
2. Get a daily devotional book to read before the evening meal.
3. Get an easy-to-read family Bible and keep it near the dinner table.
4. Invite Godly Christians to visit in your home.
5. Buy good Christian music and listen to it.
6. Put Scripture plaques on your walls.

---

1. Hebrews 11:1.
2. Proverbs 10:2.
3. Proverbs 17:13.
4. Proverbs 16:8.

BE A MAN OF DISCERNMENT!

Discernment is the ability to make accurate evaluations based on the wisdom and understanding of Scriptural principles. If you are to be successful as a man, husband, father, businessman, and spiritual leader, you must have and use spiritual discernment. You must learn how to discern the motives behind words, actions, and attitudes—not to condemn but to help and protect.

1. DISCERN WHY A PERSON WOULD REJECT THE INSPIRATION OF THE BIBLE

- ### BECAUSE A MAN WITHOUT GOD'S SPIRIT CANNOT UNDERSTAND SPIRITUAL TRUTH

   "But the natural man receiveth not the things of the Spirit of God: for they are foolishness unto him: neither can he know them, because they are spiritually discerned."[1]

   "For what man knoweth the things of a man, save the spirit of man which is in him? even so the things of God knoweth no man, but the Spirit of God."[2]

- ### BECAUSE A MAN WITHOUT MORAL PURITY WILL BE OPEN TO "THEOLOGY" WHICH EXCUSES IT

   "Wherefore God also gave them up to uncleanness through the lusts of their own hearts, to dishonor their own bodies between themselves: Who changed the truth of God into a lie, and worshipped and served the creature more than the Creator...."[3] (Humanism)

   "A man that is an heretic after the first and second admonition reject; knowing that he that is such is subverted, and sinneth, being condemned of himself."[4]

- ### BECAUSE A MAN WHO KNOWS AND REJECTS THE TRUTH ABOUT MORALITY WILL BELIEVE A LIE

   "Because that, when they knew God, they glorified him not as God, neither were thankful; but became vain in their imaginations, and their foolish heart was darkened. Professing themselves to be wise, they became fools."[5]

   "And for this cause God shall send them strong delusion, that they should believe a lie: that they all might be damned who believed not the truth, but had pleasure in unrighteousness."[6]

   "Yea, they have chosen their own ways, and their soul delighteth in their abominations. I also will choose their delusions, and will bring their fears upon them...."[7]

A MAN'S MORALITY WILL DICTATE HIS THEOLOGY

1. I Corinthians 2:14.
2. I Corinthians 2:11.
3. Romans 1:24-25.
4. Titus 3:10-11.
5. Romans 1:21-22.
6. II Thessalonians 2:11-12.
7. Isaiah 66:3-4.

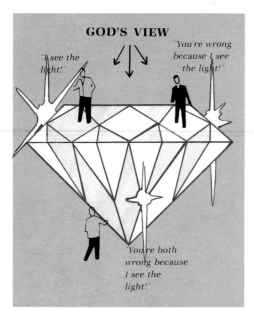

GOD'S VIEW

"I see the light!"

"You're wrong because I see the light!"

"You're both wrong because I see the light!"

A diamond reflects light from each surface. When sincere Christians differ on a teaching, it is often true that each one is focusing on a part of the truth. God's basic truths are balanced by other truths. Truth out of balance leads to heresy.

The wise Christian will pray for wisdom in order to help each one see God's balance and to correct error.

"For there must be also heresies among you, that they which are approved may be made manifest among you."[1]

DO NOT BE PRESSURED FOR ANSWERS

• If you do not know the answer, tell them that you will attempt to find the answer.

• If they want to argue over heresy, listen for clues to their moral problems.

• If they ask a foolish or unlearned question, avoid it.

• If a scorner challenges God's Word, ask him a question to prick his own conscience.

At a Christian youth camp, a proud teen-ager challenged the leader to prove that the Bible was without error. The teen-ager loved to argue about this.

The youth leader asked him a question. "Let's just suppose that for one week you did believe every word of the Bible and lived by it. Would you need to make some changes in your life?"

The teen-ager laughed and said, "I sure would have to make some changes."

The youth leader then said, "So it's not really a question of whether or not the Bible is true, but whether or not you want to change your way of living."

The teen-ager opened his mouth to say something, but nothing came out. Finally he turned to his friend and said, "He faked me out!"

1. I Corinthians 11:19.

---

2. DISCERN WHAT QUESTIONS AND DISCUSSIONS ABOUT THE BIBLE YOU SHOULD AVOID

● **DO NOT ARGUE ABOUT THEOLOGY**

"Study to shew thyself approved unto God, a workman that needeth not to be ashamed, rightly dividing the word of truth. But shun profane and vain babblings: for they will increase unto more ungodliness. And their word will eat as doth a canker [gangrene]...."[1]

"And the servant of the Lord must not strive; but be gentle unto all men, apt to teach, patient, in meekness instructing those that oppose themselves; if God peradventure will give them repentance to the acknowledging of the truth."[2]

● **DO NOT TRY TO ANSWER "FOOLISH" QUESTIONS**

"But foolish...questions avoid, knowing that they do gender strifes."[3]

A foolish question is an absurd question which has no real answer. An example of such a question is, "If God is all-powerful, why can't He make an object bigger than He can move?" The question destroys the basis upon which it is built. It is foolish speculation.

● **DO NOT TRY TO ANSWER "UNLEARNED" QUESTIONS**

"But foolish and unlearned questions avoid...."[3]

An unlearned question has an answer, but we cannot comprehend it with our human minds. God's wisdom and understanding are far above ours. If we could understand God, we would be equal with Him. An example of an unlearned question is, "What is the exact time of Christ's return?"[4] God tells us that no man knows this answer. Those who have tried to set dates have only proven that they are "unlearned."

● **DO NOT TRY TO REPROVE A SCORNER**

"He that reproveth a scorner getteth to himself shame: and he that rebuketh a wicked man getteth himself a blot. Reprove not a scorner, lest he hate thee...."[5]

"...A scorner heareth not rebuke."[6]

● **DO NOT ANSWER A FOOL ACCORDING TO HIS FOLLY**

A fool is one who said in his heart that there is no God.[7] He has ruled out the supernatural. If you try to answer him on his own philosophical level, he will not let you refer to the supernatural. When you do, he will reject you. Paul experienced this when he reasoned with the philosophers on Mars Hill.[8] Rather than trying to answer a fool on an intellectual level, show him the moral and spiritual foolishness of his position.

"Answer not a fool according to his folly, lest thou also be like unto him. Answer a fool according to his folly, lest he be wise in his own conceit."[9]

1. II Timothy 2:15-17.
2. II Timothy 2:24-25.
3. II Timothy 2:23.
4. Mark 13:32.
5. Proverbs 9:7-8.
6. Proverbs 13:1.
7. Psalm 14:1.
8. Acts 17:18-32.
9. Proverbs 26:4-5.

3. DISCERN WHEN SUBTLE ATTACKS ARE BEING MADE ON GOD'S WORD

If you want to be a wise and effective protector of your wife and children, you must learn how to recognize subtle attacks on the Bible and refute them. Just as one who whispers against you can separate you from your best friend, so one who "whispers" against the Bible can plant devastating doubts in the minds of your wife and children.

● **SUBTLE ATTACKS THROUGH "SCIENCE"**

Science is based on human observation and testimony. It is a system of measurements and weights. It formulates theories based on the laws which it can observe and reproduce in the laboratory. But what about the events before man began to observe? What about the supernatural events which cannot be recreated in the laboratory? What about the unseen powers of the spirit world?

These only become a problem to science when humanistic scientists make the false assumption that only what they can measure and weigh is reality. God warns about this kind of deceptive reasoning. He states that there will be some who scoff at realities beyond the limit of their own understanding.[1]

These people demand indisputable visible proof in order to believe the Bible. Yet God observes, "...If they hear not Moses and the prophets, neither will they be persuaded, though one rose from the dead."[2]

● **SUBTLE ATTACKS THROUGH "CULTURE"**

In our day of "women's liberation," "equal authority" for husbands and wives, and "freedom of sexuality," the clear teachings of Christ, Paul, and Peter are of particular embarrassment to religious leaders who want to be friends with the world.

Their solution is to explain that the New Testament writers were "influenced" by the culture of their day and that we must "translate" their writings into the culture of our day.

● **SUBTLE ATTACKS THROUGH "EXEGESIS"**

Exegesis is rightly interpreting the words of Scripture. Certain rules of exegesis must be followed. These rules of scholarship were designed to avoid error, but these same rules in the hands of false teachers can be misused to make a verse give an opposite meaning or no meaning at all. This is why true interpretation goes beyond human scholarship to the teaching ministry of the Holy Spirit.

Sound doctrine is based on trying the spirit, the statements, and the fruit of the teacher.[3]

1. Jude 1:10.
2. Luke 16:31.
3. I John 4:1-2; Matthew 7:20.

"The Bible is not a book about science. It is only accurate when it deals with redemption."

This attack on the inspiration of the Bible was made by a "religious" leader. The logic of his attack breaks down in many points, including the fact that "science" and redemption cannot be separated. For example, the virgin birth of Christ would involve both science and redemption.

IF SCIENCE AND THE BIBLE DISAGREE, THEN SCIENTISTS DO NOT YET HAVE ALL THE FACTS!

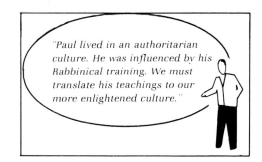

"Paul lived in an authoritarian culture. He was influenced by his Rabbinical training. We must translate his teachings to our more enlightened culture."

This attack on the authority of the Bible is the basis of many new religious books and sermons. It makes changing human culture a greater authority than the Bible.

"We can't really be sure that Paul is against sexual fantasies. The text is not conclusive on that point..."

False teachers can use a show of intellectual scholarship to distort or deny the truth of Scripture.

BE A MAN OF SPIRITUAL POWER

USE THE WORD OF GOD TO CONQUER THE POWER OF SATAN IN YOUR LIFE AND IN YOUR FAMILY

The reason that Satan does not want you to believe in the inspiration of Scripture is that he does not want you to use the Word against him as Christ did! As long as he can get you to doubt it or even defend it, he is safe. But now, let's learn how to use the Word of God to conquer Satan's power.

● **THE SINS OF THE MIND**

Your Secret Motives — Satan's Suggestions

LUSTS
Lusts of the Eyes

DESIRES
Lusts of the Flesh

AMBITIONS
Pride Of Life[15]

1. Lusts
2. Desires
3. Ambitions

1. REALIZE THAT SATAN IS YOUR CONSTANT ENEMY[1]

● When you are tempted with impure thoughts.
● When you experience doubts about God or the Bible.
● When you feel discouraged and ready to give up.
● When you are prompted to lie or gossip.
● When you hate a certain person.
● When you have fear and worry.

"For we wrestle not against flesh and blood, but against principalities, against powers, against the rulers of the darkness of this world, against spiritual wickedness in high places."[2]

When Satan plants a suggestion in your mind, you probably will not think that it came from him. You will think that it is your idea, because it satisfies the secret lusts and desires that you are allowing to remain in your heart. This is why it is so important to cleanse your heart by meditating on God's Word.[16]

2. RECOGNIZE THAT SATAN ATTACKS YOU BY PLANTING HIS SUGGESTIONS IN YOUR MIND

● Our secret thoughts are not hidden.[3]
● Satan soon learns of your secret ambitions, motives, intentions, and longings.[4]
● Satan also knows your weaknesses and when you are most vulnerable.[5]
● On the basis of this knowledge, he plants evil suggestions in your mind.[6]
● You do not usually recognize the suggestions as from Satan, because they are what you really want! By using your own wrong desires, Satan gets you to think that his ideas are really your ideas![7]

THE SINS OF THE FATHERS

"...Both I and my father's house have sinned...."[17]

God's people also "...confessed their sins, and the iniquities of their father."[18]

By acknowledging that our fathers have broken God's laws, we do not gain forgiveness for them. We recognize our responsibility to reject and avoid those same ways.

It is important to know the failings of our fathers because the sins of the fathers are visited "...upon the children unto the third and fourth generation of them that hate me."[19]

---

3. LEARN HOW TO RESIST SATAN IN YOUR MIND[7]

● Detect and reject any love for this world's ways, approval, or applause. "...Whosoever therefore will be a friend of the world is the enemy of God."[8]
● Humble yourself by submitting to your God-given authorities and confessing all past sin.[9]
● Submit yourself to obey the promptings of His Holy Spirit and to live by His power.[10]
● Resist the devil by God's Word when he plants any suggestions in your mind.[11]
● Draw near to God after the temptation in order to detect and confess the selfish motive which he used for the temptation.[12]

---

1. I Peter 5:8.
2. Ephesians 6:12.
3. Matthew 13:19.
4. James 1:14.
5. Matthew 26:41.
6. Acts 5:3.
7. II Corinthians 10:4-5.
8. James 4:4.
9. James 4:6.
10. James 4:7; Galatians 5:16.
11. James 4:7.
12. James 4:8-11.
13. Galatians 6:7.
14. Numbers 32:23.
15. I John 2:15-17.
16. Psalm 119:11.
17. Nehemiah 1:6.
18. Nehemiah 9:2.
19. Exodus 20:5.

4. BECOME SKILLFUL IN CONQUERING SATAN BY THE WORD OF GOD

The only offensive weapon that God has given to us is the Word of God. The Bible is "the sword of the Spirit."[5] As we are in right relationship with the Spirit of God and are walking by His prompting, we can expect him to bring God's Word to our mind for use against Satan's temptation.

● **STAND AGAINST SATAN IN THE NAME OF THE LORD JESUS CHRIST AND THROUGH HIS BLOOD**

When you use the name and the blood of the Lord Jesus Christ, you remind Satan that he is already defeated because of what Christ accomplished on the cross. You identify with Christ and His righteousness, not your own. You become an official representative of Christ's power and authority, not your own. Satan trembles at the name and the blood of the Lord Jesus Christ.

"And they overcame him by the blood of the Lamb, and by the word of their testimony...."[6]

● **WITHSTAND SATAN BY THE WORD OF GOD**

When Satan tempted Christ in the wilderness, Christ repeatedly used the words of Scripture to resist him. We must follow his example.

HOW DID MICHAEL CONTEND WITH THE DEVIL?

"Yet Michael the archangel, when contending with the devil...said, The Lord rebuke thee."[1]

Michael continued to contend with the devil by giving him Scriptural truth: "And the Lord said unto Satan, The Lord rebuke thee, O Satan; even the Lord that hath chosen Jerusalem rebuke thee..."[2]

Similarly, Christ resisted the devil by quoting basic Scriptures in response to specific temptations: "And when the tempter came to him...he answered and said, It is written..."[3]

---

1. SATAN'S TEMPTATION	2. YOUR RESPONSE TO SATAN	3. YOUR RESPONSE TO GOD
SATAN USES OUR DESIRES: "But every man is tempted, when he is drawn away of his own lust, and enticed."[4]	**RECOGNIZE SATAN AND RESIST HIM:** "...Resist the devil and he will flee from you."[7]	**CLEAR YOUR CONSCIENCE AND PURIFY YOUR SECRET DESIRES** "Draw nigh to God, and he will draw nigh to you. Cleanse your hands, ye sinners; and purify your hearts, ye double-minded."[8]
OUR DESIRE: To be rich **SATAN'S TEMPTATION:** To steal money	*"Lord, rebuke Satan for tempting me to steal, for it is written, 'Thou shalt not steal.'[9] I ask this in the name and through the blood of the Lord Jesus Christ."*	*"Lord, I realize that Satan was able to tempt me because I have a secret love of money. I confess this to You and ask You to forgive me and cleanse me from this sin."*
OUR DESIRE: To enjoy impurity **SATAN'S TEMPTATION:** To lust after a woman	*"Lord, I ask You in the name and through the blood of the Lord Jesus Christ, to rebuke Satan for tempting me to lust after that woman, for it is written, '...whosoever looketh on a woman to lust after her hath committed adultery with her already in his heart.'"[10]*	*"Heavenly Father, I realize that Satan was able to tempt me to lust after that woman, because I have a secret desire to enjoy immorality. I ask you to cleanse my heart from this wicked desire, and give me the grace to learn genuine love."*

---

1. Jude 9.
2. Zechariah 3:2.
3. Matthew 4:3-4.
4. James 1:14.

5. Ephesians 6:19.
6. Revelation 12:11.
7. James 4:7.
8. James 4:8.

9. Exodus 20:15.
10. Matthew 5:28.
11. Philippians 3:8.

TWELFTH WEEK:

☐ Study pages 63-64.
☐ Complete Application No. 12.
☐ Develop Quality No. 4 (page 6).

QUESTION No. 12

Why is it so important for me and my family to live under the authority of the Bible?

ANSWER:

When you live under the authority of the Bible, you establish the basis for your own leadership. Your authority does not come from yourself. It is given to you by God for God's purposes. It is very important for you to be able to explain all your decisions on the basis of God's Word. As your family accepts the Bible, they will accept the basis of your decisions.

QUIZ No. 12 **CAN YOU GIVE GOD'S ANSWERS ON INSPIRATION?**

(Match God's answers with questions on inspiration.)

QUESTIONS ON INSPIRATION

GOD'S ANSWERS ON INSPIRATION

1. Is the Word of God essential for salvation?

A. ☐ "All Scripture is given by inspiration of God..." (II Timothy 3:16).

2. How highly did God exalt His own Word?

B. ☐ "For the prophecy came not in old time by the will of man: but holy men of God spake as they were moved by the Holy Ghost" (II Peter 1:21).

3. Has God preserved the accuracy of the Bible?

C. ☐ "...Man shall not live by bread alone, but by every word that proceedeth out of the mouth of God" (Matthew 4:4).

4. Did Christ do away with Old Testament law?

D. ☐ "...Thou hast magnified thy word above all thy name" (Psalm 138:2).

5. Was the entire Bible given by inspiration?

E. ☐ "Every word of God is pure..." (Proverbs 30:5). "The words of the Lord are pure words: as silver tried in a furnace of earth, purified seven times" (Psalm 12:6).

6. Is every word of the original manuscript pure?

F. ☐ "And it is easier for heaven and earth to pass, than one tittle of the law to fail" (Luke 16:17).

7. Why is the Bible so essential to daily living?

G. ☐ "Think not that I am come to destroy the law, or the prophets: I am not come to destroy, but to fulfill" (Matthew 5:17).

8. Was it man's idea to write out the Bible?

H. ☐ "...When ye received the word of God which ye heard of us, ye received it not as the word of men, but as it is in truth, the word of God..." (I Thessalonians 2:13).

9. Did the early Christians believe in inspiration?

I. ☐ "Being born again, not of corruptible seed, but of incorruptible, by the word of God which liveth and abideth forever" (I Peter 1:23).

10. Why do some people reject inspiration?

J. ☐ "And for this cause God shall send them strong delusion, that they should believe a lie: That they all might be damned who believed not the truth but had pleasure in unrighteousness" (II Thessalonians 2:11-12).

PROVIDE COPIES FOR YOUR FAMILY.

APPLICATION No. 12

1. Purpose to bring your entire family under the authority of the Bible.

Thy law, O Lord, is perfect, converting my soul. Thy testimonies are sure, making wise the simple. Thy statutes are right, rejoicing my heart. Thy commandment is pure, enlightening my eyes.[1]

2. Examine your previous attitudes toward the authority of the Bible. Think through the questions on page 31 and ask forgiveness of God and your family for anything which you have done to damage their trust in God's Word.

3. Identify any seeds of doubt or reaction which your family may have to the authority of God's Word. Study the questions on page 25.

4. Discern the causes of rebellion to the Bible. Study page 26.

5. Take wise and loving steps to remove any rebellion to God's Word. Work out the quiz on page 28.

6. Memorize ten Scripture verses on inspiration.

☐ Speak with authority by memorizing the verses listed on the opposite page.

☐ Ask your wife to help you memorize them. She can assist you by writing or typing each verse out on a 3" x 5" card so that you can carry them with you throughout the day and work on them during spare moments. An excellent time to memorize is while going to and from work.

☐ Set a goal for completing the verses (see page 63).

☐ Ask your wife to check the verses you have memorized. Learn to quote them perfectly. The mental struggles which you may have in memorizing the verses "word perfect" will be a living demonstration to your wife and family that you really do want God's best in your life, whatever the cost.

7. Give your family the quiz on inspiration.

☐ Explain the quiz on the opposite page. Each person is to match the best verse with the question on inspiration. Write the number of the question in the appropriate box.

☐ **QUIZ ANSWERS:**

1. I	3. F	5. A	7. C	9. H
2. D	4. G	6. E	8. B	10. J

---

1. Personalization of Psalm 19:7-8.

QUESTION No. 13

How can I instruct my family to reject any counsel which is contrary to the Bible?

ANSWER:

You can teach your family to reject counsel which is contrary to the Bible by teaching them how to evaluate your counsel on the basis of God's Word. The apostle Paul praised the Berean Christians because they "searched the Scriptures daily"[1] to see whether Paul's teaching was true to the Word of God.

A wise father will encourage his family to do the same with the teaching and counsel which he gives. In order to do this, a man must clearly understand from the Bible the scope and limitations of his responsibilities.

QUIZ No. 13   CAN YOU MAKE WISE AND RESPECTFUL APPEALS?

IF YOUR FATHER SAID...

ON WHAT SCRIPTURE VERSE WOULD YOU BASE YOUR APPEAL?

1. "Ask your pastor that question. I don't know much about the Bible."

2. "I don't know how to solve all my problems. Don't expect me to know everything."

3. "Don't look at me that way. I have a right to get angry, if I want to."

4. "I'll go to church, but your mother is the religious one in the family."

5. "Don't think that a man isn't a Christian just because he isn't born again."

6. "You shouldn't need any spankings. I'm going to expect you to always be good without them."

7. "You should learn to be on your own. You just have to try out some things for yourself."

8. "Put your mother in a rest home and let the government take care of her."

9. "Your mother and I have lost our love for each other. Don't you agree that this is why I have to leave her?"

A. ☐ "Jesus answered and said unto him, Verily, verily, I say unto thee, except a man be born again, he cannot see the kingdom of God" (John 3:3).

B. ☐ "If any of you lack wisdom, let him ask of God, that giveth to all men liberally, and upbraideth not; and it shall be given him" (James 1:5).

C. ☐ "Study to show thyself approved unto God, a workman that needeth not to be ashamed, rightly dividing the word of truth" (II Timothy 2:15).

D. ☐ "Husbands, love your wives, even as Christ also loved the church, and gave himself for it; that he might sanctify and cleanse it with the washing of water by the word" (Ephesians 5:25-26).

E. ☐ "And these words, which I command thee this day, shall be in thine heart: and thou shalt teach them diligently unto thy children..." (Deuteronomy 6:6-7).

F. ☐ "Withhold not correction from the child..." (Proverbs 23:13). "...For what son is he whom the father chasteneth not?" (Hebrews 12:7).

G. ☐ "But if any provide not for his own, and especially for those of his own house, he hath denied the faith, and is worse than an infidel" (I Timothy 5:8).

H. ☐ "Where no counsel is, the people fail: but in the multitude of counsellors there is safety" (Proverbs 11:14).

I. ☐ "...Let every man be swift to hear, slow to speak, slow to wrath: for the wrath of man worketh not the righteousness of God" (James 1:19-20). "...And, ye fathers, provoke not your children to wrath..." (Ephesians 6:1-4).

PROVIDE COPIES FOR YOUR FAMILY.

1. Acts 17:10-11.

APPLICATION No. 13

1. Purpose to teach your family how to detect and reject counsel which is contrary to the principles of God's Word.

> "...Let God be true, but every man a liar..."[1]
> "...Nevertheless the counsel of the Lord, that shall stand."[2]

2. Encourage your family to see the Scriptural basis of your counsel.

☐ Determine that all your instruction will be consistent with the Biblical authority which God has entrusted to you as a father. Assure your family that you would never want them to follow any counsel which is contrary to the Word of God, and that if you ever gave such counsel, you would want them to respectfully appeal to you on the basis of Scripture.

3. Establish your Scriptural responsibilities.

☐ Explain that God has given the following responsibilities to every father, and that your statements and actions must be consistent with these responsibilities.

A. To be a "growing" Christian (John 3:3).
B. To depend on God's wisdom for decisions (James 1:5).
C. To diligently study the principles of God's Word (II Timothy 2:15).
D. To love your wife as Christ loved the Church (Ephesians 5:25-26).
E. To teach your children the principles of God's Word (Deuteronomy 6:6-7).
F. To correct your children in love (Proverbs 29:17; 23:13; Hebrews 12:7).
G. To provide for your family (I Timothy 5:8).
H. To protect your family (I Peter 5:8-9).
I. To be loving and patient in all that you do (James 1:19; Ephesians 6:1-4).

4. Introduce the quiz on making Scriptural appeals.

☐ Ask each family member to match the father's statements with the best Scripture verse.

☐ **QUIZ ANSWERS:**

1. E	3. I	5. A	7. H	9. D
2. B	4. C	6. F	8. G	

5. Explain how to summarize verses in a respectful appeal.

☐ Express acceptance and understanding of what the father has said.
A. "I respect your opinion about what a Christian is...."
B. "I can understand how you feel about not knowing...."
C. "I'm sure there are reasons why you would tell me to...."

☐ Explain how much it would mean to you for your father to follow God's way.

A. "...It would mean so much to me for you to...."
B. "...I would really be grateful if you would...."

☐ Share what God states "with meekness and reverence."

1. Romans 3:4.   2. Proverbs 19:21.

85

FOURTEENTH WEEK:

☐ Study pages 65-67.
☐ Complete Application No. 14.
☐ Identify Quality No. 5 (page 6).

QUESTION No. 14

How can I be sure that I have the correct interpretation of a verse of Scripture?

ANSWER:

God states that "rightly dividing the Word of truth" comes by study—your study and the guiding insights of the Holy Spirit.[1]

In the study of the Bible, it is important to remember that there is only one interpretation of a verse,[2] but there are many applications of it to daily living. It is exciting to have the Holy Spirit reveal practical applications of a Scripture verse, but we can be sure that His applications are not in conflict with any other verse or truth of Scripture.

Paul illustrated how one verse has more than one application. In I Timothy 5:18, and also in I Corinthians 9:9, he emphasizes the importance of giving an adequate salary to ministers. In order to reinforce his point, he quotes an Old Testament verse which at first appears to have no relationship to a minister: "Thou shalt not muzzle the ox when he treadeth out the corn."[3]

Obviously, this verse must be interpreted in relation to the ox. Yet there is an underlying principle which has application for us today. "Doth God care for oxen [only]? Or saith he it altogether for our sakes [too]? For our sakes, no doubt...."[4]

A further important aid to study is being able to look up the precise meanings of key words in their original language. This can be done with a complete concordance.

QUIZ No. 14   CAN YOU MATCH THE GREEK ALPHABET?

PROVIDE COPIES FOR YOUR FAMILY.

	GREEK NAME	CAPITAL LETTER	SMALL LETTER	MATCH THE ENGLISH EQUIVALENT	
1	Alpha . . .	A	α	d	—
2	Beta . . .	B	β	e̅	—
3	Gamma . .	Γ	γ	z	—
4	Delta . . .	Δ	δ	b	2
5	Epsilon . .	E	ε	a	1
6	Zeta . . .	Z	ζ	g	—
7	Eta . . .	H	η	th	—
8	Theta . .	Θ	θ	e	
9	Iota . . .	I	ι	l	—
10	Kappa . .	K	κ	x	—
11	Lambda . .	Λ	λ	p	—
12	Mu . . .	M	μ	i	—
13	Nu . . .	N	ν	o	—
14	Xi	Ξ	ξ	k	—
15	Omicron .	O	o	n	—
16	Pi . . .	Π	π	m	
17	Rho . . .	P	ρ	u	—
18	Sigma . .	Σ	σ	ch	—
19	Tau . . .	T	τ	o̅	—
20	Upsilon . .	Y	υ	r	—
21	Phi . . .	Φ	φ	t	—
22	Chi . . .	X	χ	ps	—
23	Psi . . .	Ψ	ψ	ph	—
24	Omega . .	Ω	ω	s	—
				TOTAL	

● **THE NEXT STEP IS TO USE A GREEK-ENGLISH DICTIONARY.**

1. John 16:13.   2. II Peter 1:20, 21.   3. Deuteronomy 25:4.   4. I Corinthians 9:9, 10.

APPLICATION No. 14

1. Purpose to teach your family how to look up key New Testament words in a Greek-English dictionary.

> *"I will study to show myself approved unto God, a workman that needeth not to be ashamed, rightly dividing the Word of Truth."*[1]

2. Purchase a concordance of the Bible which contains Hebrew and Greek dictionaries in the back. This large volume will be an invaluable aid to you and your family in studying the Bible.

3. Become familiar with the concordance. Read the instructions on page 65 of this Manual. Look up the word "private" in your own concordance.

4. Become familiar with the Greek alphabet.

5. Introduce your family to the Greek alphabet.

- ☐ The quiz on the opposite page is a fun way to introduce your family to the Greek dictionary in the concordance.
- ☐ Begin by asking, "Who knows where the word 'alphabet' came from?" (The first two words of the Greek alphabet.)
- ☐ "The New Testament was written in Greek. If we knew Greek, we could learn all the little extra shades of meaning that are lost in the English translation of the Bible."
- ☐ "Let's learn how to look up key New Testament words in a Greek-English dictionary, but first let's see if you can match up the Greek alphabet with the English alphabet."
- ☐ "I'll give you a clue. The English letters between the lines can be matched to the Greek letters between the same lines."
- ☐ "Everyone wins in this project, because what you learn now will be valuable to you for the rest of your lives."

ANSWERS TO QUIZ: GREEK MATCHED TO ENGLISH EQUIVALENT					
GREEK	**ENGLISH**	**GREEK**	**ENGLISH**	**GREEK**	**ENGLISH**
1.	a (5)	9.	i (12)	17.	r (20)
2.	b (4)	10.	k (14)	18.	s (24)
3.	g (6)	11.	l (9)	19.	t (21)
4.	d (1)	12.	m (16)	20.	u (17)
5.	e (8)	13.	n (15)	21.	ph (23)
6.	z (3)	14.	x (10)	22.	ch (18)
7.	ē (2)	15.	ō (13)	23.	ps (22)
8.	th (7)	16.	p (11)	24.	o (19)

6. Show your family how to look up "private" in the concordance.

- ☐ If time allows, have each one look up a key word, such as inspiration, Scripture, prophecy, delusion.
- ☐ Encourage them to use the concordance in their own study of the Bible.
- ☐ Looking up words in the original language will give more and more confidence and accuracy in interpreting Scripture.

---

1. Personalization of II Timothy 2:15.

QUESTION No. 15

If I am responsible for the leadership of my family, how can I always be sure that my decisions are right?

ANSWER:

First, make sure that every decision is in harmony with the basic principles of Scripture. Second, test every decision against the commands of Scripture, the testimonies of Scripture, the counsel of your authorities, and the inward peace of the Holy Spirit.

Illustrate these points to your family through the following quiz.

QUIZ No. 15   **A SYMBOLICAL MEAL**

CAN YOU IDENTIFY WHAT EACH COURSE REPRESENTS?

First Course: **GELATIN MOLDS** (all different molds)
Clue #1 - Notice the gelatin molds. Each one is different.

1. _____

Second Course: **CELERY STALKS**
Clue #2 - Celery must be kept under cover for a while; otherwise, it will be bitter.

2. _____

Third Course: **POTATOES** (any style)
Clue #3 - A potato is a root grown in the dark, but later it comes into the light.

3. _____

Fourth Course: **WHEAT BREAD**
Clue #4 - The grain of wheat must die before it brings forth a harvest for bread.

4. _____

Fifth Course: **LEMON WEDGE** and **CRANBERRY JUICE**
(choose one for each person)
Clue #5 - These are bitter, but they have cleansing qualities in them. You didn't choose the one you received.

5. _____

Sixth Course: **UNLEAVENED BREAD**
(crackers with no yeast)
Clue #6 - These crackers have no yeast. In the Bible, yeast is a type of sin.

6. _____

Seventh Course: **STEAK or MILK**
Clue #7 - This product comes from a cow. A cow is a "clean" animal because its hoof is divided and it chews its cud.

7. _____

PROVIDE COPIES FOR YOUR FAMILY.

APPLICATION No. 15

1. Purpose that you are going to make wise and accurate decisions as the spiritual leader of your family.

> *"Teach me thy way, O Lord, and lead me in a plain path, because of mine enemies."*[1]

2. Work together with your wife on a symbolic meal.

☐ Give the quiz on the opposite page.

☐ After the meal, read the answers. (Each course represents a basic Scriptural principle.)

Clue #1: **DESIGN:** God made each one of us with a different "mold." It was chosen for us for our spiritual growth.

Clue #2: **AUTHORITY:** If we are not under the protective covering of God's authority, we will become bitter.

Clue #3: **RESPONSIBILITY:** We must be sure that our secret life is pleasing to God, because it will be exposed to the light someday. The effectiveness of our service to others will be based on our ability to clear up "root problems."

Clue #4: **OWNERSHIP:** We must die to our rights and possessions; otherwise, we "abide alone." When we "let go" of our things, God works through them to bring life to others.

Clue #5: **SUFFERING:** Suffering is bitter, but if responded to properly, it will bring cleansing and healing to us and to others. God chooses the suffering best suited for us.

Clue #6: **FREEDOM:** God wants our lives to be free of sin and moral impurity. Only then will we represent the body and life of the Lord Jesus.

Clue #7: **SUCCESS:** Meditation on the Word is compared to a cow ruminating on its cud. The chewing of the cud by a cow produces milk and meat. The meditation of a Christian allows him to enjoy the milk and the meat of God's Word.

NOTE: These statements are true because they are commands in the Bible, and because they are in harmony with the principles of God's Word. Scripture alone can be misused by Satan.[2]

3. Learn to apply this four-fold test to all your decisions.

A. THE TEST OF SCRIPTURAL COMMANDS

A decision is never right if it violates a direct or an indirect command of Scripture. It would be a wrong decision to form a close friendship with an immoral man who claims to be a Christian.[3] It would be a wrong decision to labor in order to be rich.[4] It would be an unwise decision to form a business partnership with equal control.[5]

B. THE TEST OF SCRIPTURAL ILLUSTRATIONS

God promises to make us wiser than all our teachers if we meditate on His testimonies. Relive the biographies which He has written. Watch for cause and effect sequences. For example, ask yourself what Abraham, Isaac, and Jacob could have done differently to have avoided the personal and family conflicts which they experienced. Look in Scripture for a situation comparable to the one which you are now facing.

C. THE TEST OF PROPER COUNSEL

God has placed us under authorities so that we can enjoy the benefit and protection of their wisdom and experience. We are not to forsake the counsel of our father or mother when they are old.[6] A husband is also wise to hold off a decision as long as possible if his wife is not in full harmony with it.

D. THE TEST OF GOD'S SPIRIT

A wrong decision may look right, but if we are alert to the prompting of God's Spirit, we will not have His peace in the matter. You should have inward peace after the first three tests have been passed. "Let the peace of God rule [be the umpire] in your hearts."[7]

---

1. Psalm 27:11.   3. I Corinthians 5:11.   5. Matthew 6:24.   7. Colossians 3:15.
2. Luke 4:10-11.   4. Proverbs 23:4.   6. Proverbs 23:22.

QUESTION No. 16

How can I learn to delight myself in the Lord so that He will give me the desires of my heart?

ANSWER:

You can learn how to delight yourself in the Lord by learning how to meditate on God's Word day and night. When a father commits himself to do this, he will be forced to rearrange his priorities and his schedule around the Word. Meditation is essential to the success of each one in your family. It is very important to teach them how to do it.

QUIZ No. 16   HOW DOES A PERSON DELIGHT IN THE LORD?

(Match the questions to the best Scriptural answer.)

QUESTIONS:

1. How much of God's Word must we delight in if we want God's prosperity?

2. To what degree must we give ourselves to God's Word if we want to meditate on it?

3. What requirements does God put on His "holy day" if we want to delight in Him?

4. How will our bedtime meditation influence our ability to find satisfaction?

5. Does God promise success in everything we do if we delight in His Word day and night?

6. Can rejection from others motivate us to delight more deeply in God's Word?

7. How will delighting in God's testimonies influence our ability to be wise?

GOD'S ANSWERS

A. ☐ "But his delight is in the law of the Lord; and in his law doth he meditate day and night...Whatsoever he doeth shall prosper" (Psalm 1:2-3).

B. ☐ "My soul shall be satisfied...when I remember thee upon my bed, and meditate on thee in the night watches" (Psalm 63:5-6).

C. ☐ "I have more understanding than all my teachers: for thy testimonies are my meditation" (Psalm 119:99).

D. ☐ "Princes also did sit and speak against me: but thy servant did meditate in thy statutes" (Psalm 119:23).

E. ☐ "If thou turn away thy foot from...doing thy pleasure on my holy day...then shalt thou delight thyself in the Lord..." (Isaiah 58:13-14).

F. ☐ "...Thou shalt meditate therein day and night, that thou mayest observe to do according to all that is written therein: for then thou shalt make thy way prosperous..." (Joshua 1:8).

G. ☐ "Meditate upon these things; give thyself wholly to them; that thy profiting may appear to all" (I Timothy 4:15).

	TRUE	FALSE	
8.	☐	☐	Meditation is "opening up our subconscious mind" to thoughts of God.
9.	☐	☐	We should begin our day in the morning by meditating on God's Word.
10.	☐	☐	If we meditate day and night, we will be successful in everything we do.
11.	☐	☐	We will always sleep peacefully if we begin meditating on God's Word.

APPLICATION No. 16

1. Purpose to teach your family how to delight in the Lord by meditating on His Word day and night.

O Lord, I will delight myself in You and in Your Word, so that You can give me the desires that should be in my heart.[1]

2. Experience the discipline and delight of a "night watch."

☐ A man who delights in fishing will get up early in the morning to fish. A young man who delights in a girl will think about her day and night. David applied this same kind of delight to God's Word. He woke up during the night to meditate on God's Word. God called David a man after His own heart.[2]

☐ "At midnight I will rise to give thanks unto thee...."[3] "Mine eyes prevent [I woke up before] the night watches, that I might meditate in thy Word."[4]

☐ Set your alarm for the middle of the night (with your wife's permission). Read Psalm 119:47-112, Psalm 63, and Psalm 5. Memorize Psalm 63:5-6 and meditate on it as you go back to sleep.

3. Give your family the quiz on delighting in the Lord.

☐ **QUIZ ANSWERS:**

1. F	3. E	5. A	7. C
2. G	4. B	6. D	

4. Teach your family the eight steps of meditation (pages 69-70).

5. Summarize your teaching with the true or false quiz.

TRUE AND FALSE ANSWERS:

8. FALSE. Meditation is not thinking our thoughts about God. It is transforming our thoughts by God's Word.[5]

9. FALSE. We should begin our day in the evening with meditation. God made the day to begin in the evening.[6] Our last thoughts at night will influence our night and the next day.

10. TRUE. We will prosper in whatever we do.[7] One reason for this is that God's Word will direct us away from wrong people and unfruitful projects.

11. TRUE AND FALSE. Meditation will help us get to sleep faster and give us a better sleep, but at first, God's Word may "dislodge" impure thoughts which are hidden in our minds. This may cause "unpleasant dreams" until our minds are purified by God's Word.[8]

---

1. Personalization of Psalm 37:4
2. I Samuel 13:14
3. Psalm 119:62
4. Psalm 119:148
5. Romans 12:2
6. Genesis 1:5
7. Psalm 1:2-3
8. John 15:3

☐ Study pages 71-74.
☐ Complete Application No. 17.
☐ Identify Quality No. 6 (page 6).

QUESTION No. 17

How can I understand what is really happening in this complex world?

ANSWER:

You can begin to understand what is really happening in the world by interpreting news items in the light of Biblical prophecy and in the light of basic Scriptural truths.

When men do not understand something, or when they do not want others to understand something, they make it sound very complex. But God turns complex problems into easily-understood answers so that everyone can deal with them according to the principles of His Word.

In order to understand what is happening in our world, we must understand God's overall program. We must then check every statement that we hear, using the basic truth of Scripture as a guide.

Deceptive statements contain error or partial truths which are designed to produce false conclusions. If we believe false ideas, we are deceived. If we act on them, we reap destruction.

QUIZ No. 17

HAVE YOU BEEN DECEIVED?

COMMON IDEAS AND STATEMENTS	TRUE	FALSE	IF FALSE, CAN YOU EXPLAIN?
1. It is the job of the government to provide an education for all children.	☐	☐	☐
2. A strong nation is built on strong local communities.	☐	☐	☐
3. A child's personality cannot be changed after seven.	☐	☐	☐
4. Every culture has the right to make up its own standards of morality.	☐	☐	☐
5. Primitive tribes are emerging from the "stone age."	☐	☐	☐
6. Man is becoming more advanced.	☐	☐	☐
7. Truth is not something you find, but something you keep searching for.	☐	☐	☐
8. A newspaper should report all the facts it gets, because "the public has a right to know."	☐	☐	☐
9. News reporting, like history writing, can and should be done with an objective mind.	☐	☐	☐
10. Criminals are really victims of our society.	☐	☐	☐
11. Alcoholism is a disease.	☐	☐	☐
12. What a man eats is what a man becomes.	☐	☐	☐
13. The key to good health is good food, good sleep, and good exercise.	☐	☐	☐
14. The history of mankind is simply a continual repetition of itself.	☐	☐	☐

PROVIDE COPIES FOR YOUR FAMILY.

APPLICATION No. 17

1. Purpose to identify and expose deceptive statements of worldly philosophies and to teach your children how to interpret the true meaning of world events.

Lord, I will beware, lest any man spoil me or my family through vain philosophy and vain deceit, after the rudiments of men, after the rudiments of the world, and not after Christ.[1]

2. Determine how much deception you have already been exposed to. Give the quiz on the preceding page to your family. Make sure that you have sufficient time to discuss the answers. If possible, have your children write out why the statements are false. Have them check their answers with yours. Remember, false statements can be partially true.

ANSWERS TO QUIZ:

1. **FALSE:** Education of children is primarily the responsibility of the father, not the government.[2] No facts of life should be taught apart from their relationship to God and to His moral standards. The teachers the father hires must reinforce the Godly instruction that he gives.[3] There is no such thing as a "neutral education." Either it is Godly, or Godless.

2. **FALSE:** A strong nation is built on strong families. When the "community" is emphasized rather than the family, the social problems that develop are beyond the power of a democracy to solve. The democracy must then become a dictatorship. Families then lose their freedom to worship God, because the dictator becomes the new "god."[4]

3. **FALSE:** The "learned behavioral patterns" of a person which do not conform to the character of Christ can be changed at any age.[5]

4. **FALSE:** God has established universal moral standards which no nation can violate without experiencing the resulting consequences.[6]

5. **FALSE:** "Primitive tribes" are not the result of lack of education. They are the remnants of great and advanced civilizations which rejected God's moral laws.[7]

6. **FALSE:** Man's knowledge is increasing, but man is becoming more and more corrupt and sinful as we approach the end times.[8]

7. **FALSE:** Truth can and must be found in order to have eternal life and temporal success. "Ye shall know the truth and the truth shall make you free."[9] Jesus is the way and the truth.[10]

8. **FALSE:** Truth out of balance leads to error. Incomplete facts or facts put in a negative light promote false conclusions in the minds of the readers. Detrimental information about people should never be made public until all the facts have been checked out privately.[11] It is never right for a public news media to violate God's moral standards.[12]

9. **FALSE:** No person can be truly "objective" or free from his own bias. In the very reporting of news or history, the reporter must look for certain facts and leave out other facts. He will be influenced by his own experience and philosophy of life.[13] Reporters should use facts to emphasize the truths of God's Word, not as "neutral information."

10. **FALSE:** Criminals are not the victims of social injustice. They are only demonstrating the basic sin nature which is in every person who is not controlled by the power of Christ.[14] The unregenerate heart is deceitful and wicked.[15]

11. **FALSE:** Alcoholism is not a disease. It is a type of sin. Its Scriptural name is "drunkenness."[16]

12. **FALSE:** A person is not what he eats, but what he thinks. "For as he thinketh in his heart, so is he."[17] Because of this, we must guard our heart and mind with all diligence.[18]

13. **FALSE:** The key to good health is not just food, or sleep, or exercise, but Godliness.[19] A person's health is influenced more by guilt and bitterness than by food, sleep, or exercise.

14. **FALSE:** History is not continuous repetition. It is God's program for man built around the person of Jesus Christ. There is a beginning and an ending. Within this structure there are repeated lessons to mankind about Christ and His standards of living. History is "His story."[20]

3. Explain the basic events of prophecy. (See material on pages 72-74.)

1. From Colossians 2:8.
2. Deuteronomy 4:9; 6:6-7; Proverbs 1:8, 2:1.
3. Galatians 4:1-2.
4. The history of Israel.
5. II Corinthians 5:17.
6. Ephesians 5:3-6.
7. Romans 1.
8. II Timothy 3:1-6.
9. John 8:32.
10. John 14:6.
11. Deuteronomy 19:16-19; Proverbs 25:8-9.
12. Exodus 20:16; Ephesians 5:12.
13. Matthew 12:33-35.
14. Romans 3:9-19.
15. Jeremiah 17:9.
16. Proverbs 23:21; I Corinthians 5:11.
17. Proverbs 23:7.
18. Proverbs 4:23.
19. I Timothy 4:8.
20. Hebrews 1, 2.

QUESTION No. 18

How can I teach my family to avoid arguments over religion and philosophy?

ANSWER:

You can teach your family to avoid arguments about religion and philosophy by teaching them how to discern the real reasons why people reject God's truth and by teaching them how to detect the various types of attitudes which cause arguments.

FIVE TYPES OF FOOLS WHO ARGUE

God gives precise definitions of wrong character based on the Hebrew words. He wants us to love everyone but to learn how to respond wisely to wrong attitudes.

TYPES OF FOOLS	HOW SHOULD WE RESPOND?
1. **THE "SIMPLE FOOL"** *(pᵉthîy)*[1] He is without knowledge and easily seduced.	He needs to be instructed. We should try to help him.
2. **THE "REACTIONARY FOOL"** *('ĕvîyl)*[2] He simply wants his own way.	He needs to be disciplined. We should direct him to his authorities.
3. **THE "SILLY FOOL"** *(kᵉcîyl)*[2] He is only interested in a good time.	He needs major reproofs. We should explain his error and go from his presence.
4. **THE "SCORNING FOOL"** *(lûwts)*[3] He has rejected truth and delights in mocking Christians and their standards.	He will hate a reprover and blot his name. Get away from him.
5. **THE "COMMITTED FOOL"** *(nâbâl)*[2] He is the victim of his own passions.	He is committed to teaching you. Reject his teachings. Have no association with him.

CAN YOU IDENTIFY THESE TYPES OF FOOLS FROM PROVERBS?

		WHICH TYPE OF FOOL IS THIS?
A.	He believes every word that people tell him. (14:15)	☐
B.	Every child is born with this type of foolishness. (22:15)	☐
C.	He hates anyone who reproves him. (9:8)	☐
D.	He is not to be answered according to his folly. (26:4)	☐
E.	He has said in his heart, "There is no God." (Psalm 14:1)	☐
F.	He appears to be wise if he doesn't talk. (17:28)	☐
G.	He poses as a religious leader. (Ezekiel 13:3)	☐
H.	He destroys the morals of his companions. (13:20)	☐
I.	He doesn't foresee danger and suffers for it. (22:3)	☐
J.	He becomes cunning when scorners are punished. (19:25)	☐
K.	He seeks wisdom but doesn't find it. (14:6)	☐
L.	He wants to "discover his heart," not understanding. (18:2)	☐
M.	He belittles the danger of sin. (14:9)	☐
N.	He does not even hear rebuke. (13:1)	☐
O.	He is obnoxious to everyone around him. (24:9)	☐
P.	His complacency destroys the simple fool. (1:32)	☐
Q.	Contentions cease when he is cast out. (22:10)	☐
R.	He requires punishment by civil authorities. (19:29)	☐
S.	He believes sin is right because it is popular. (Psalm 92:6-7)	☐
T.	He can learn wisdom from Proverbs. (1:4)	☐

1. Hebrew word for "simple."   2. Hebrew word for "fool."   3. Hebrew word for "scorner."

PROVIDE COPIES FOR YOUR FAMILY.

APPLICATION No. 18

1. Purpose to train your family how to avoid arguments over religion and philosophy.

Your servant, O Lord, "Must not strive; but be gentle unto all men, apt to teach, patient, in meekness instructing those that oppose themselves: if God peradventure will give them repentance to the acknowledging of the truth."[1]

2. Explain the quiz on the five types of fools who argue.

Explain how important it is to be able to discern the types of attitudes within those who want to argue with us. If we answer a "simple fool," we may help him, and he will be eternally grateful to us. If we try to answer a "scorning fool," he won't listen. He will hate us and we will get a blot to our name.

Go over the five types of fools, and then have your family see how many of the types they can identify. Reward the winner. (Total points from both quizzes.)

ANSWERS:

A (1)	E (5)	I (1)	M (2)	Q (4)
B (2)	F (1)	J (1)	N (2-5)	R (3-5)
C (4)	G (5)	K (4)	O (4)	S (3)
D (3)	H (3-5)	L (3)	P (3)	T (1)

3. Apply what you have learned in the following quiz.

Explain that you will give an argumentative statement. They are to write down how they would respond to the arguer. After they write down all their responses, read the answers.

ARGUMENTATIVE STATEMENT:	HOW WOULD YOU RESPOND?
1. I think it would be fun to visit a prostitute (Prov. 7:7).	(1-Try to warn him.)
2. My father thinks that I am wrong (Prov. 15:5).	(2-Direct him back to his father.)
3. I despise my mother (Prov. 15:20).	(3-Tell him he is wrong and leave.)
4. I'm forming a group to confront the boss (Prov. 22:10).	(4-Don't reprove him. Get away.)
5. God wants us to have sexual openness (Ezek. 13:3).	(5-Reject his teachings. Leave.)
6. You can't really find wisdom and truth (Prov. 14:6).	(4-Don't reprove him. Get away.)
7. I hate that man for preaching at me (Prov. 15:12).	(4-Don't reprove him. Get away.)
8. You have got to have some fun in life (Prov. 18:2).	(3-Tell him he is wrong and leave.)
9. How can you prove there is a God (Ps. 14:1)?	(5-Reject his teaching. Leave.)

4. Explain further insights.

☐ A person who does not believe in God is like a person who eats lots of candy and does not believe in dentists. Just give him a little time.

☐ The way a son or daughter responds to a father is the same way that he or she will tend to respond to God.[2] Clearing up disbelief in God cannot be done without also clearing up rebellion toward the father.

☐ Two types of people get involved in false cults. Those who have never heard the truth and those who have rejected the truth. We should try twice to talk to those who have never heard the truth.[3]

☐ The key to witnessing is listening—listening for the "cracks" in another man's life, marriage, family, and business. "Listening" is like rubbing your spiritual finger along the edge of that man's life and feeling for the "cracks," and then helping him to find God's answers.

☐ The three tests of sound doctrine are testing the spirit of the person and his words, testing the statements against all of Scripture, and testing the fruit of a person's message and life.[4]

1. Personalization of II Timothy 2:24-25.
2. Malachi 4:6.
3. Titus 3:10-11.
4. I John 4:1-2; Matthew 7:20.

QUESTION No. 19

How can I recognize the things in my home which are hindering the Word of God?

ANSWER:

You can recognize things in your home which are hindering the Word of God by asking your wife and family to identify everything which violates Scripture or hinders their fellowship with the Lord. After removing these, bring into your home those things which will encourage spiritual growth. Then, have a special service to dedicate your home to the Lord.

WHY DO UNNECESSARY FAMILY TRAGEDIES HAPPEN?

1. **God's curse upon the father (Deuteronomy 7:25-26).**
2. **Satan's destruction of a man's family (Mark 3:27).**
3. **A wicked fellow seducing a man's daughter (II Timothy 3:1-6).**
4. **A father being disqualified from church leadership (I Timothy 3:11).**

QUIZ No. 19   **HAVE YOU CLEANSED YOUR HOME?**

(Match the items to cleanse with the Scriptural references.)

ITEMS TO CLEANSE	SCRIPTURE REFERENCES
1. Pornographic books, magazines, or other sensual material.	A. ☐ "For rebellion is as the sin of witchcraft, and stubbornness is as iniquity and idolatry" (I Samuel 15:23).
2. Statues, images, charms, heathen gods of false worship, etc.	B. ☐ "...For of this sort are they which creep into houses, and lead captive silly women laden with sins, led away with divers lusts..." (II Timothy 3:6).
3. Books, material, or objects related to horoscopes, fortune telling, ouija boards, etc.	C. ☐ "The graven images of their gods shall ye burn with fire...neither shalt thou bring an abomination into thine house, lest thou be a cursed thing like it: but thou shalt utterly detest it, and thou shalt utterly abhor it; for it is a cursed thing" (Deuteronomy 7:25-26).
4. Music which expresses the philosophy of rebellion to authority and moral standards.	D. ☐ "...Inquire not after their gods, saying, How did these nations serve their gods..." (Deuteronomy 12:30).
5. Books by false religions or cults.	E. ☐ "But I say unto you, that whosoever looketh on a woman to lust after her hath committed adultery with her already in his heart" (Matthew 5:28).
6. Rebellious or immoral friends; lovers of pleasure more than lovers of God; those who are proud and disobedient to parents.	F. ☐ "Therefore shall evil come upon thee...the astrologers, the stargazers, the monthly prognosticators ...shall be as stubble..." (Isaiah 47:11-14).

APPLICATION No. 19

1. Purpose to recognize the things in your home which are hindering the Word of God, and remove them.

"I will walk within my house with a perfect heart. I will set no wicked thing before mine eyes...He that worketh deceit shall not dwell within my house...."[1]

2. Discuss with your wife the items which she feels are hindering the spiritual growth of the family. Agree together to remove the items which belong to you. Work together in prayer and exhortation to convince your sons and daughters to remove the items which belong to them. Begin this entire project by asking God to bind Satan in the name and through the blood of the Lord Jesus Christ so that you can regain the spiritual ground which he has been given.

3. Explain to your family the great importance of having God's blessing upon your home. Read the following statements and ask different family members to read the accompanying verses.

☐ Evil things in the home bring God's curse upon the father (Deuteronomy 7:25-26).
☐ If the father is bound by any evil thing, Satan can destroy his house (Mark 3:27).
☐ Lack of standards allows wicked men to creep in and seduce daughters (II Timothy 3:6).
☐ If evil is rewarded for good, evil will not depart from the family (Proverbs 17:13).
☐ Rebellion in the home disqualifies the father from church leadership (I Timothy 3:4, 5-12).
☐ Godless influences stifle a father's ability to teach God's principles (Deuteronomy 6:7).

4. Share with your family the idea of a "Dedication Dinner."

☐ "Let's cleanse our home of everything which displeases the Lord, and then we will invite our pastor over to dedicate our home to the Lord."

5. Give the quiz on cleansing your home.

QUIZ ANSWERS:

1. E	3. F	5. D
2. C	4. A	6. B

6. After removing all the items which you know are contrary to the Word of God, replace them with items which you know will build spiritual growth.

A. GOOD CHRISTIAN MUSIC in the home. This is tremendously important for setting a Godly atmosphere. Cheerful Gospel music could be used to begin the day. Melodious music should be played before mealtimes. (Many arguments take place during the hour before a meal.) Devotional music could be played in the evening before bedtime. Change the music often.

B. A LARGE TYPE, SELF-PRONOUNCING BIBLE put near your dinner table.

C. A GOOD DAILY DEVOTIONAL GUIDE which suggests a portion of Scripture to read and gives a commentary on its application to daily living. Perhaps the most effective time to read the passage of Scripture and the commentary is just before the meal. Then thank God for His Word and for the meal.

D. BIOGRAPHIES of the great men and women in God's "Hall of Fame." Read and discuss them with your family.

E. ATTRACTIVE SCRIPTURE PLAQUES, table mats, and items which have significance because of answered prayer or spiritual lessons learned.

---

1. Psalm 101:2, 3-7.

QUESTION No. 20

How can I learn to overcome the power of temptation in my life?

ANSWER:

God has given clear steps of action on how to resist the devil so that he will flee from us. "...God...giveth grace to the humble. Submit yourselves therefore to God. Resist the devil, and he will flee from you. Draw nigh to God, and he will draw nigh to you. Cleanse your hands, ye sinners; and purify your hearts, ye double-minded. Be afflicted, and mourn, and weep...humble yourselves in the sight of the Lord, and he shall lift you up."[1]

QUIZ No. 20   DO YOU KNOW HOW TO CONQUER SATAN'S POWER?

(Match the best explanation with each step. Watch for clues.)

SCRIPTURAL STEPS	MATCHING EXPLANATIONS
1. Identify the problem.	A. ☐ This means to get under God's authority. We must cease to be our own "boss" by proclaiming Jesus Christ as our Savior and Lord. Then we must submit to God's Word and obey the promptings of His Holy Spirit.[2]
2. Get more grace.	B. ☐ This involves two steps: First, recognize the ideas, suggestions, and impulses which the Devil has put in your mind; then ask God to rebuke Satan in the name and through the blood of the Lord Jesus Christ.[3]
3. Submit to God.	C. ☐ God explains that every person is tempted "when he is drawn away of his own lust, and enticed."[4] This problem means that our temptations are actually signals that we have secret desires and motives which are against God's will.[5]
4. Resist the Devil.	D. ☐ We cannot conquer temptation with our own will power. God must give us the desire and the power to do His will. This is the true meaning of God's grace.[6]
5. Draw near to God.	E. ☐ This requires that we search out the hidden motives and longings of our heart. Surface temptations are often clues to secret desires which we have allowed to remain in our innermost heart.[7]
6. Cleanse your hands.	F. ☐ This means to see our wretched condition before God. Then we will have the proper motivation to afflict our soul with true fasting, prayer, and repentance.[8]
7. Purify your heart.	G. ☐ This step is necessary if we want Satan to stay away once he flees from us. God allows Satan to tempt us so that we will see our need to come near to Him.[9]
8. Be afflicted.	H. ☐ Satan uses past sins to bring new temptations. It is essential to confess these sins and ask forgiveness of God and of those who were offended. When we cleanse our conscience, we are given new power over temptation.[10]
9. Humble yourself in God's sight and He will lift you up!	I. ☐ Each of the above steps requires humility on our part. As we sincerely humble ourselves in God's sight, He will give us the power to overcome Satan.[11]

1. James 4:6-10.
2. Romans 10:9-10; 12:1-2; 13:1-6; 16:17-19.
3. Matthew 16:23; Jude 1:9.
4. James 1:14.
5. James 4:1-5.
6. Titus 2:11-12.
7. Jeremiah 17:9-10.
8. Matthew 5:4.
9. Psalm 27:7-8.
10. I Timothy 1:19.
11. I Peter 5:6.

PROVIDE COPIES FOR YOUR FAMILY.

98

APPLICATION No. 20

1. Purpose to use the power of God to overcome the power of Satan in your life and in your family.

O Lord, sin shall not have dominion over me, because greater are You who is in me than he that is in the world.[1]

2. Illustrate the steps of conquering Satan's temptations.

1. Identifying the problem:	Satan brings a temptation to our mind such as to tell a lie, to steal, or to commit immorality.
2. Getting more grace:	In ourselves, we do not have the ability to conquer these temptations. If we use human effort to resist them, we will face a bigger temptation of pride.
3. Submitting to God:	God gives us the desire and the power (grace) to overcome temptation if we are under His authority. This involves receiving His salvation, dedicating our lives to Christ and God's Word, and being obedient to parents and other human authorities.
4. Resisting the Devil:	When we recognize that these temptations are from Satan, we must ask God to rebuke him, and then we must quote the Scripture that relates directly to the temptation.

> *Heavenly Father, I ask You to rebuke Satan, in the name and through the blood of the Lord Jesus Christ, for tempting me to (lie), (steal), (be immoral), because it is written (thou shalt not bear false witness),[2] (thou shalt not steal), (sin shall not have dominion over you).[4]*

5. Drawing near to God:	Satan will flee when we resist him, but he will quickly return unless we allow God to reveal the hidden causes of the temptation.
6. Cleansing our hands:	The first thing Satan uses for new temptations is our past sin—lies we told, things we stole, acts of immorality. These must be confessed and made right.
7. Purifying our own heart:	Even if we clear our conscience, Satan can still tempt us by hidden desires which are contrary to God's will. (A desire for the praise of men will bring temptations to lie or deceive; the love of money will bring temptations to steal or covet; a longing to satisfy the lusts of the flesh will bring temptations to be immoral).
8. Being afflicted:	True repentance comes as we see the true condition of our deceitful heart. We must ask God to search our heart and reveal every hidden desire that is grieving His Holy Spirit.[5]
9. Humbling ourselves:	As we take these steps, we will experience more and more of the power of God and the character of Christ, so that our desires will no longer be controlled by Satan, but by Christ.

3. Memorize James 4:4.

"Ye adulterers and adulteresses, know ye not that the friendship of the world is enmity with God? Whosoever therefore will be a friend of the world is the enemy of God."

4. Give the quiz on conquering Satan's power to your family.

☐ Explain that this is a difficult quiz because several explanations could match several different steps. However, they should choose the best explanation for each step. As a clue, each step and the matching explanation have the same key word. The value of the quiz is in thinking through the steps and the explanations.

☐ **QUIZ ANSWERS:**

1. C (Clue Word: PROBLEM)	5. G (Clue Word: NEAR)
2. D (Clue Word: GRACE)	6. H (Clue Word: CLEANSE)
3. A (Clue Word: SUBMIT)	7. E (Clue Word: HEART)
4. B (Clue Word: DEVIL)	8. F (Clue Word: AFFLICT)
	9. I (Clue Word: HUMBLE)

1. Personalization of Romans 6:14 and I John 4:4.   4. Romans 6:14.
2. Exodus 20:16.   5. Psalm 139:23.
3. Exodus 20:15.

APPLICATION No. 21

1. Purpose to become skillful in defeating Satan with the sword of the Spirit.

Lord, above all, I will take the shield of faith and the sword of the Spirit, which is Your Word.[1]

QUIZ No. 21

HOW SKILLFUL ARE YOU WITH THE SWORD OF THE SPIRIT?

The "sword of the Spirit is the Word of God" (Ephesians 6:17). When Jesus was tempted by Satan (Matthew 4:3-4), He demonstrated how to overcome him by quoting precise verses of Scripture. Can you match the precise verse with each temptation?

TEMPTATION		PRECISE SCRIPTURE
1. Look on a woman with lust.	A. ☐	"Obey them that have the rule over you, and submit yourselves: for they watch for your souls, as they that must give account, that they may do it with joy, and not with grief..." (Hebrews 13:17).
2. Learn false philosophies.	B. ☐	"...My son, despise not thou the chastening of the Lord, nor faint when thou art rebuked of him: For whom the Lord loveth he chasteneth..." (Hebrews 12:5-6).
3. Envy sinners.	C. ☐	"Do all things without murmurings and disputings" (Philippians 2:14).
4. Tell a lie.	D. ☐	"...Thou shalt meditate therein day and night, that thou mayest observe to do according to all that is written therein: for then thou shalt make thy way prosperous..." (Joshua 1:8).
5. Murmur.	E. ☐	"Be [careful] for nothing; but in every thing by prayer and supplication with thanksgiving let your requests be made known unto God" (Philippians 4:6).
6. Gossip about an enemy.	F. ☐	"Lie not one to another..." (Colossians 3:9).
7. Neglect meditation.	G. ☐	"...Whosoever looketh on a woman to lust after her hath committed adultery with her already in his heart" (Matthew 5:28).
8. Despise parents' restrictions.	H. ☐	"Let not thine heart envy sinners: but be thou in the fear of the Lord all the day long. For surely there is an end; and thine expectation shall not be cut off" (Proverbs 23:17-18).
9. Worry over finances.	I. ☐	"Not rendering evil for evil, or railing for railing: but contrariwise blessing..." (I Peter 3:9).
10. Resent God's correction.	J. ☐	"Beware lest any man spoil you through philosophy and vain deceit, after the tradition of men, after the rudiments of the world, and not after Christ" (Colossians 2:8).

PROVIDE COPIES FOR YOUR FAMILY.

1. Personalization of Ephesians 6:16-17.

2. Review how Christ conquered Satan by quoting precise Scripture.

☐ Read Christ's temptation in Matthew 4:1-11.

☐ Introduce the quiz on quoting precise Scriptures.

QUIZ ANSWERS:

1. G	3. H	5. C	7. D	9. E
2. J	4. F	6. I	8. A	10. B

3. Stress the importance of purifying our heart of secret desires.

"But every man is tempted, when he is drawn away of his own lust, and enticed" (James 1:14).

"I the Lord search the heart, I try the reins, even to give every man according to his ways, and according to the fruit of his doings" (Jeremiah 17:10).

4. Identify the types of hidden desires, motives, ambitions, longings, and lusts which give Satan the freedom to bring related temptations.

☐ Love of the "world": The lust of the flesh, the lust of the eyes, and the pride of life.

"Love not the world, neither the things that are in the world. If any man love the world, the love of the Father is not in him" (I John 2:15).

☐ Love of money

"For the love of money is the root of all evil..." (I Timothy 6:10).

☐ Desire for revenge

"But if ye forgive not men their trespasses, neither will your Father forgive your trespasses" (Matthew 6:15).

5. Explain how Satan uses our secret desires to defeat us.

Satan uses our hidden desires as the basis to plant his suggestions and reasonings in our minds and make us think that they are our own ideas. Our "double mind" or secret longings, also make our prayers for deliverance ineffective. "But let him ask in faith, nothing wavering. For he that wavereth is like a wave of the sea driven with the wind and tossed. For let not that man think that he shall receive any thing of the Lord. A double minded man is unstable in all his ways."[1]

It is not easy to purify our hearts because "The heart is deceitful above all things, and desperately wicked: who can know it?"[2] For this reason we must spend time before the Lord and ask Him to search our hearts. "...I am he which searcheth the reins and hearts: and I will give unto every one of you according to your works."[3]

Our heart attitude in the presence of the Lord will tell Him how sincere we are in purifying our double-mindedness. This is why He instructs us to "Be afflicted, and mourn, and weep: let your laughter be turned to mourning, and your joy to heaviness. Humble yourselves in the sight of the Lord, and he shall lift you up."[4]

If we are sincere, the Holy Spirit will reveal the secret desires of our heart which Satan is using as the basis for our temptations. These desires will be related to our love of the things of this world. "Ye adulterers and adulteresses, know ye not that the friendship of the world is enmity with God? Whosoever therefore will be a friend of the world is the enemy of God...."[5]

When the Holy Spirit reveals our hidden motives, God will give us the grace (desire and power) to purify our hearts as we humble ourselves. "But he giveth more grace. Wherefore he saith, God resisteth the proud, but giveth grace unto the humble."[6]

---

1. James 1:6-8. 4. James 4:9-10.
2. Jeremiah 17:9. 5. James 4:4-5.
3. Revelation 2:23. 6. James 4:6.

LEARN TO BE SKILLFUL WITH GOD'S WORD

SATAN INFLUENCING YOUR EYES.

SATAN INFLUENCING YOUR TONGUE.

SATAN'S TEMPTATIONS	SATAN'S DECEPTIONS
1. Look on a woman with lust.	You are only fulfilling a God-given desire.
2. Look at pornography.	What is wrong with having a "lust" for life?
3. Study false religions.	You can't be effective in witnessing unless you fully understand what the other person believes. <u>Note</u>: Paul illustrates the proper way to deal with false religions in I Corinthians 15:12-58. He pinpoints their error in only one verse and explains the truth in forty five verses.
4. Learn false philosophies.	You won't be educated unless you know them.
5. Give your parents a look of disgust.	Your parents need to be reminded that you are old enough to make your own decisions.
6. Envy sinners.	Look at all the fun you are missing.
7. Tell a lie.	You will lose respect if you tell people the truth about yourself.
8. Murmur about your work.	You might be able to bring about changes if you express enough discontent.
9. Complain about a physical handicap.	You should let people know what you must live with. If God loved you, He wouldn't have let that happen to you.

Follow Christ's example of using precise verses of Scripture when Satan comes with specific temptations.

GOD'S TRUTH	OUR SECRET MOTIVES
It is written: "...Whosoever looketh on a woman to lust after her hath committed adultery with her already in his heart" (Matthew 5:28).	To fulfill the lust of the eyes. (See I John 2:15-17.)
It is written: "For whosoever will save his life [for his own pleasure] shall lose it: and whosoever will lose his life for my sake shall find it" (Matthew 16:25). "...Make not provision for the flesh, to fulfill the lusts thereof" (Romans 13:14).	To make provision for the lusts of the eyes and of the flesh. (See I John 2:15-17.)
It is written: "Cease, my son, to hear the instruction that causeth to err from the words of knowledge" (Proverbs 19:27). "...I would have you wise unto that which is good, and simple concerning evil" (Romans 16:19).	To fulfill the pride of learning. To be like God, knowing good and evil. (See Genesis 3:5.)
It is written: "Go from the presence of a foolish man, when thou perceivest not in him the lips of knowledge" (Proverbs 14:7). "Beware lest any man spoil you through philosophy and vain deceit, after the tradition of men, after the rudiments of the world, and not after Christ" (Colossians 2:8).	To fulfill the pride of knowledge. Being ashamed of the simplicity of the Gospel of Christ. (See II Corinthians 11:3.)
It is written: "The eye that mocketh at his father, and despiseth to obey his mother, the ravens of the valley shall pick it out, and the young eagles shall eat it" (Proverbs 30:17).	To reject authority and be your own boss. (See I Samuel 15:23.)
It is written: "Let not thine heart envy sinners: but be thou in the fear of the Lord all the day long. For surely there is an end; and thine expectation shall not be cut off" (Proverbs 23:17-18).	To find "acceptable" ways of enjoying the pleasures of sin. (See Hebrews 11:25.)
It is written: "Lie not one to another..." (Colossians 3:9). "...[Satan] is a liar, and the father of it" (John 8:44).	To gain the praise of men rather than the approval of God. (See Proverbs 18:12.)
It is written: "Do all things without murmurings and disputings" (Philippians 2:14).	To get your own way. To avoid God's disciplines. (See Philippians 2:5-9.)
It is written: "In every thing give thanks: for this is the will of God in Christ Jesus concerning you" (I Thessalonians 5:18).	To get sympathy and attention at the expense of God's glory. (See II Corinthians 12:8-10.)

SATAN'S TEMPTATIONS	SATAN'S DECEPTIONS
10. Give a bad report about another Christian.	You need to warn others about this person.
11. Judge another person.	You can't change them, so why try?
12. Gossip about someone who falsely accused you.	You must teach him what it feels like when people damage your reputation.
13. Use profanity.	You need to use that language if you really want to get your point across.
14. Question the accuracy of the Bible.	You can't really be sure about a book that was written so long ago by so many different men.
15. Become too busy for daily Bible reading.	It won't hurt you to miss a few days.
16. Put off memorization.	You don't need to memorize. You'll get just as much out of a verse if you read it.
17. Neglect meditation.	You have other things to think about before you meditate. Besides, you can't remember any verse to meditate on.

GOD'S TRUTH	OUR SECRET MOTIVES
It is written: "Speak not evil one of another, brethren..." (James 4:11). "Brethren, if a man be overtaken in a fault, ye which are spiritual, restore such an one in the spirit of meekness; considering thyself, lest thou also be tempted" (Galatians 6:1).	To fulfill the pride of appearing to be better than others. (See Matthew 18:15.)
It is written: "Judge not, that ye be not judged. For with what judgment ye judge, ye shall be judged..." (Matthew 7:1-2).	To condemn in others what you cannot conquer in yourself. (See Romans 2:1-3).
It is written: "Not rendering evil for evil, or railing for railing: but contrariwise blessing..." (I Peter 3:9). "Dearly beloved, avenge not yourselves, but rather give place unto wrath: for it is written, Vengeance is mine; I will repay, saith the Lord" (Romans 12:19).	To get revenge for what he did to you. (See Romans 12:21).
It is written: "Thou shalt not take the name of the Lord thy God in vain..." (Exodus 20:7). "Let no corrupt communication proceed out of your mouth, but that which is good to the use of edifying..." (Ephesians 4:29).	To express anger and establish your own authority. (See I Peter 3:10).
It is written: "All scripture is given by inspiration of God..." (II Timothy 3:16). "Heaven and earth shall pass away: but my words shall not pass away" (Mark 13:31).	To be free from the authority of the Bible and its standards of morality. (See II Thessalonians 2:10-12).
It is written: "...Man shall not live by bread alone, but by every word that proceedeth out of the mouth of God" (Matthew 4:4).	To avoid the fact that you have lost your first love for the Lord and His Word. (See Revelation 2:4).
It is written: "Thy word have I hid in mine heart, that I might not sin against thee" (Psalm 119:11).	To excuse mental laziness and a lack of diligence in seeking God. (See Proverbs 22:17-18).
It is written: "...Thou shalt meditate therein day and night, that thou mayest observe to do according to all that is written therein: for then thou shalt make thy way prosperous..." (Joshua 1:8).	To exercise pride in deciding what you will use your mind to think about. (See I Timothy 4:15).

SATAN'S TEMPTATIONS	SATAN'S DECEPTIONS
18. Despise the restrictions of your parents or pastor.	You are entitled to your own opinion on these personal matters.
19. Satisfy curiosity in learning about the occult.	It won't hurt you to learn about it. Maybe you can use your knowledge to counsel others to avoid it.
20. Plan to profit at another's expense.	You have a right to make all the money you can. You must look out for "Number One."
21. Worry over financial pressures.	You can't count on God to help you. If He was concerned, He would not have allowed the situation to get so bad.
22. Be discouraged with the Christian life.	You have failed so many times so why try any more?
23. Fear the future.	It is normal to fear the unknown.
24. Feel inferior.	You would be much happier if you could look like someone else.
25. Resent God's correction.	If God really loved you, He wouldn't allow so much trouble to come into your life.

GOD'S TRUTH	OUR SECRET MOTIVES
It is written: "Obey them that have the rule over you, and submit yourselves: for they watch for your souls, as they that must give account, that they may do it with joy, and not with grief: for that is unprofitable for you" (Hebrews 13:17).	To be your own boss and enjoy the things of the world. (See James 4:1-6).
It is written: "There shall not be found among you any one ...that useth divination, or an observer of times [horoscopes]... for all that do these things are an abomination unto the Lord..." (Deuteronomy 18:10-12).	To be like God knowing good and evil with your mind. (See Genesis 3:5).
It is written: "Thou shalt not steal" (Exodus 20:15). "Treasures of wickedness profit nothing..." (Proverbs 10:2). "A good name is rather to be chosen than great riches..." (Proverbs 22:1).	To gratify the love of money. (See I Timothy 6:9-11).
It is written: "And having food and raiment let us be therewith content" (I Timothy 6:8). "Be [anxious] for nothing; but in every thing by prayer and supplication with thanksgiving let your requests be made known unto God" (Philippians 4:6).	To be able to depend on your resources rather than on God's resources. (See I Timothy 6:6-10).
It is written: "...Let us not be weary in well-doing: for in due season we shall reap, if we faint not" (Galatians 6:9).	To please God with what you can do rather than draw strength from what He has done through Christ. (See II Corinthians 15:10).
It is written: "For God hath not given us the spirit of fear; but of power, and of love, and of a sound mind" (II Timothy 1:7).	To assume that God will punish you in the future for past sins. (See I John 1:9).
It is written: "...Measuring themselves by themselves, and comparing themselves among themselves, [they] are not wise" (II Corinthians 10:12). "I will praise thee; for I am fearfully and wonderfully made..." (Psalm 139:14).	To gain the admiration of people rather than the approval of God. (See Matthew 5:16).
It is written: "...My son, despise not thou the chastening of the Lord, nor faint when thou art rebuked of him: For whom the Lord loveth he chasteneth..." (Hebrews 12:5-6).	To blame God for the consequences of violating His principles. (See Proverbs 19:3).

HOW DID HE TURN HIS NATION BACK TO GOD?

Elijah lived in a day when the people of his nation worshipped God with their mouths but served the gods of lust and pleasure with their hearts. How did Elijah turn his nation back to God?

First, he brought the people to a point of decision. "...How long halt ye between two opinions? if the Lord be God, follow Him: but if Baal, then follow him...."[1]

Second, he revealed the futility of the lustful worship of Baal, and then he demonstrated the reality and power of the Lord. [2]

In our day as well, "...the eyes of the Lord run to and fro throughout the whole earth, to shew himself strong in the behalf of them whose heart is perfect toward him...."[3]

Every father must wisely bring each member of his family to a total commitment to God and to the principles of His Word.

1. I Kings 18:21.
2. I Kings 18:22-40.
3. II Chronicles 16:9.

4 BE STRONG!

☐ A man proves his manliness when he fulfills God-given responsibilities. One of his most important responsibilities is to instill Godly standards and Scriptural convictions in the lives of his wife, sons, daughters, and grandchildren.

☐ It is one thing to establish standards and convictions; it is another thing to maintain them. To maintain standards and convictions, a man must be strong in faith, strong in grace, and mighty in spirit.

☐ A man's wife and children want to see consistency in his life. They do not want him to be committed to God's standards at one time and not at another.

☐ To be strong is to be able to:
- Explain your convictions to your family.
- Make it exciting and rewarding for your family to learn Scriptural principles, Godly standards, and personal convictions.
- Establish and maintain God's standards in your home.
- Prepare your family to stand alone for God's principles.
- Teach your sons and daughters how to instill convictions in the lives of their children.

QUESTIONS FOR PERSONAL APPLICATION

> The following questions are amplified throughout this section and specifically answered on pages 120-131.

22 HOW CAN I REMOVE DOUBTS WHICH HINDER THE ASSURANCE OF SALVATION?

23 HOW CAN I MOTIVATE MY FAMILY TO BUILD GODLY CHARACTER INTO THEIR LIVES?

24 HOW CAN I HELP A MEMBER OF MY FAMILY ACCEPT PHYSICAL AND FAMILY DEFECTS?

25 WHAT IF MY FAMILY ASKS ME QUESTIONS ABOUT THE CHRISTIAN LIFE WHICH I DO NOT KNOW HOW TO ANSWER?

26 WHAT SHOULD I DO IF SOMEONE IN MY FAMILY REJECTS THE WORD OF GOD AND LIVES IN REBELLION?

27 WHAT COUNSEL SHOULD I GIVE MY SONS AND DAUGHTERS IF THEY ARE EVER REQUIRED TO STUDY "HUMANISTIC" PHILOSOPHIES OR A FALSE RELIGION?

4 BE STRONG IN PURPOSE!

MAINTAIN THIS CONVICTION IN YOUR OWN LIFE, AND MAKE IT EXCITING FOR YOUR FAMILY TO BUILD THEIR LIVES AROUND THE AUTHORITY OF THE BIBLE.

BE STRONG IN PURPOSE!

Be committed to the success of your wife, your children, and your grandchildren. A father's responsibility for his sons and daughters does not end when they finish school or marry. It does not end until a father goes on to be with the Lord! This is the message of God's command for fathers to teach their sons and their son's sons.[1]

The crown of a father is not his children, but his grandchildren. "Children's children are the crown of old men."[3]

- ● **LIST EACH ONE UNDER YOUR RESPONSIBILITY**

  - ☐ Your wife
  - ☐ Your sons
  - ☐ Your daughters
  - ☐ Your daughters-in-law
  - ☐ Your sons-in-law
  - ☐ Your grandsons
  - ☐ Your granddaughters
  - ☐ Your granddaughters-in-law
  - ☐ Your grandsons-in-law

> **YOUR CHILDREN'S CHILDREN TELL THE WORLD HOW SUCCESSFUL YOU WERE IN REARING YOUR CHILDREN!**

- ● **BE DILIGENT TO KNOW THEIR SPIRITUAL CONDITION[2]**

NAMES	DATE OF THEIR SALVATION	DATE OF THEIR BAPTISM	THEIR SPIRITUAL PURPOSE IN LIFE	DAILY BIBLE READING	MEMORIZING SCRIPTURE

1. Deuteronomy 4:9.
2. Proverbs 27:23.
3. Proverbs 17:6.

BE STRONG IN GRACE

"THOU THEREFORE, MY SON, BE STRONG IN THE GRACE THAT IS IN CHRIST JESUS."[4]

Grace is not "God's indulgence" in letting us do what we want to do. "What shall we say then? Shall we continue in sin that grace may abound? God forbid...."[1]

Grace is not God's removal of temporal consequences for breaking His law. "Be not deceived; God is not mocked: for whatsoever a man soweth, that shall he also reap. For he that soweth to his flesh shall of the flesh reap corruption...."[2]

Grace is not the freedom to reject God's moral laws, but the desire and power to keep them.

"...Earnestly contend for the faith...For there are certain men crept in unawares...ungodly men, turning the grace of our God into lasciviousness...."[3]

1. Romans 6:1-2.
2. Galatians 6:7-8.
3. Jude 1:3-4.
4. II Timothy 2:1.
5. John 3:16.
6. I Corinthians 15:10.
7. Romans 11:6.
8. Ephesians 2:8-9.
9. II Peter 3:18.
10. Hebrews 12:15.
11. James 4:6.
12. Titus 2:11-12.
13. Ephesians 2:4-7.

1. LEARN THE DEFINITION OF GRACE
THE DESIRE AND POWER TO DO GOD'S WILL

The grace of God is an attribute of God; however, all God's attributes are active. For example, God is love. Yet He expressed His love by giving ("God so loved...that He gave....").[5] God expresses His grace to us by giving us the desire and the power to do His will. Paul clearly emphasizes this fact.

"But by the grace of God I am what I am: and his grace which was bestowed upon me was not in vain; but I labored more abundantly than they all: yet not I, but the grace of God which was with me."[6]

Grace is free—we do not earn it.

"And if by grace, then is it no more of works: otherwise grace is no more grace. But if it be of works, then is it no more grace...."[7]

- **God gives grace (desire and power) to non-Christians to believe on the Lord Jesus Christ.**

  "For by grace are ye saved through faith; and that not of yourselves: it is the gift of God: not of works, lest any man should boast."[8]

- **God gives grace to Christians to grow in Christ.**

  "But grow in grace, and in the knowledge of our Lord and Saviour Jesus Christ...."[9]

- **God's grace can be resisted.**

  "Looking diligently lest any man fail of the grace of God...."[10]

- **God's grace is given to the humble.**

  "But he giveth more grace. Wherefore he saith, God resisteth the proud, but giveth grace unto the humble."[11]

- **God's grace gives us the desire and the power to keep God's laws—not the freedom to reject them.**

  "For the grace of God that bringeth salvation hath appeared to all men, teaching us that, denying ungodliness and worldly lusts, we should live soberly, righteously, and godly, in this present world."[12]

- **God's mercy forgives us when we fail to respond to His grace.**

  "But God, who is rich in mercy, for his great love wherewith he loved us, even when we were dead in sins, hath quickened us together with Christ, [by grace ye are saved]...That in the ages to come he might shew the exceeding riches of his grace...."[13]

2. GAIN MORE OF GOD'S GRACE BY HUMBLING YOURSELF BEFORE GOD AND YOUR FAMILY

CONFESS LACK OF SPIRITUAL LEADERSHIP

Acknowledge to God and to your family if you have not been the spiritual leader that God wanted you to be. State your desire to become a spiritual leader by getting under the authority of God's Word and making the Bible a priority in your life.

ASK FOR PRAYER

Ask your wife and children if they would pray for you and encourage you to be the spiritual leader that you should be.

ASK FORGIVENESS WHEN YOU FAIL

Expect to be judged on the basis of your consistency, especially if you have tried before and failed.

- Make a list of ways that your wife wants you to be a spiritual leader.

  - Praying with her
  - Studying the Bible with her
  - Going to church regularly
  - Answering spiritual questions
  - _____
  - _____
  - _____
  - _____

- Make a list of ways that your sons and daughters want you to lead them spiritually.

  - Praying before meals
  - Praying for them and their friends
  - Reading the Bible at dinner
  - Answering their questions and problems
  - Making mealtimes more meaningful
  - _____
  - _____
  - _____

- List the ways in which you have discouraged spiritual things in the family in the past. Ask forgiveness for them and resolve not to do them again.

  - Belittling spiritual things
  - Finding fault with Christian leaders
  - Taking God's name in vain
  - Refusing to tithe
  - Making it hard for them to go to church
  - Criticizing sermons
  - Ridiculing others who attempt to witness
  - Judging other Christians
  - Displaying a lack of enthusiasm for God's work
  - Losing your temper and displaying pride

> "BEFORE DESTRUCTION THE HEART OF MAN IS HAUGHTY, AND BEFORE HONOR IS HUMILITY."[1]

Most husbands are not aware of just how important it is to pray with their wives.

"Likewise, ye husbands, dwell with them according to knowledge, giving honor unto the wife, as unto the weaker vessel, and as being heirs together of the grace of life; that your prayers be not hindered."[2]

A further "unknown" to many husbands is the importance and potential of making their wives radiant through the Word of God.

"Husbands, love your wives, even as Christ also loved the church, and gave himself for it; That he might sanctify and cleanse it with the washing of water by the word."[3]

One of the influential and encouraging practices of a father is to pray for each one in the family, by name, before the breakfast meal.

1. Proverbs 18:12.
2. I Peter 3:7.
3. Ephesians 5:25-26.

113

3. BE ALERT TO THE DANGER OF UNANSWERED QUESTIONS ABOUT THE BIBLE

Just as a whisperer about you can alienate your best friend,[1] so a whisperer about God's Word can produce destructive doubts in the minds of your family members. You must discover what questions have been planted in their minds and work out clear Scriptural answers.

"For there are many unruly and vain talkers and deceivers...whose mouths must be stopped, who subvert whole houses, teaching things which they ought not, for filthy lucre's sake."[2]

QUESTION: Hasn't evolution proven that parts of the Bible are only myth?

ANSWER: No. Evolution is a theory based on several man-made assumptions which, by their nature, are not capable of experimental verification. There is no scientific way to prove a theory on creation because creation is not a repeatable event. Since these assumptions which support the theory of evolution can not be proven, they must be accepted by faith. Similarly, the Christian believes and understands through faith "...that the worlds were framed by the Word of God...."[3] The Christian believes the divinely revealed account of creation given to man by the Creator Himself in Genesis 1. Thus, the theory of evolution cannot disprove Genesis 1 since both must be accepted on the basis of faith.

The question is, do we put our faith in an unprovable man-made theory, or do we put our faith in the God-breathed Scriptures which Christ our Lord said, "...cannot be broken"?[4]

Evolution is a philosophy of life. It allows the one who believes in it to be his own god and to believe that he is getting better and that he will be able to work out his own problems. If evolution is wrong, then its followers become accountable to a holy God. They immediately become responsible for God's moral standards, which they have already broken.

QUESTION: Isn't evolution built on scientific fact?

ANSWER: Evolutionists are often guilty of choosing only those scientific facts which support their theory and ignoring those facts which contradict their theory. The Second Law of Thermodynamics is a good example. It summarizes the fact that in random motion (on which evolution is based) things go from order to disorder, not from disorder to order. Evolutionists say, for example, that the solar system went from disorder to order. This contradicts a basic law of physics which evolutionists have not been able to satisfactorily answer.

1. Proverbs 16:28.
2. Titus 1:10-11.
3. Hebrews 11:3.
4. John 10:35.

BE STRONG IN GOD'S SPIRIT

God wants every man to be mighty in Spirit. "...To be strengthened with might by His Spirit in the inner man."[1]

To be strong in God's Spirit means:

Sensing God's presence at all times and developing the fear of the Lord.

Recognizing the promptings of the Holy Spirit and being alert to spiritual danger.

Understanding the deeper things in God's Word.[2]

Discerning the wrong kind of attitudes and ideas in others and knowing how to respond to them.

Comprehending the height and depth of God's love.[3]

Motivating others to grow in the Lord and apply Scripture to daily living.[4]

Building your life around basic Scriptural principles and convictions.

Knowing how to "bind Satan" and rescue members of your family from his power.

JOHN THE BAPTIST

"And the child grew and waxed strong in spirit...."[6]

MOTIVATE YOUR FAMILY TO BECOME MIGHTY IN GOD'S SPIRIT

TELL THEM WHAT WILL PLEASE YOU

Children want and need the acceptance and approval of their father. Assure them of your acceptance of them just the way they are, but also tell them how they can gain your approval by their words, thoughts, and actions.

"You will make me a very happy father if you grow up being a wise person. Wisdom is more important than riches or popularity!"[5]

WORK WITH EACH ONE IN LEARNING WISDOM

If wise sons and daughters are the most important goal for you, then you will take time and effort to build wisdom into their lives. The following project is ideal for this.

"Let's work on a project together. It will give us more wisdom. Let's take the wisest proverbs in the world and rearrange them under topics."

Many fathers have already found this project to be an invaluable way of instilling wisdom and the fear of the Lord in their sons and daughters.

Plan to get up an hour early once a week and work on the project. Start with two words: "wisdom" and "fools." After gathering the verses, write out insights and personal applications.

1. Ephesians 3:16.
2. Hebrews 5:13-14.
3. Ephesians 3:18-19.
4. Hebrews 10:24.
5. Proverbs 10:1; 8:11.
6. Luke 1:80.

TOPIC: WISDOM

1:2 To know wisdom....

1:3 To receive the instruction of wisdom, justice, judgment, and equity.

1:5 A wise man will hear and will increase learning.[1]

1:7 Fools despise wisdom and instruction.

1:8 Hear the instruction of thy father.[2]

1:20 Wisdom crieth without....

2:1 If...thou incline thine ear unto wisdom...then shalt thou understand the fear of the Lord and find the knowledge of God.

2:6 For the Lord giveth wisdom....

2:7 He layeth up sound wisdom for the righteous.

2:9 Then shalt thou understand righteousness, and judgment, and equity, yea every good path.[2]

2:10 When wisdom entereth into thine heart.

PERSONAL APPLICATIONS

1. I must learn how to listen for wisdom and then write down what I learned.

2. I must listen to the right people for wisdom—starting with my father.

3. I must remember that wisdom is the key to a happy life.

GOD'S "HALL OF FAME"

THE APOSTLE PAUL

His faith and convictions led him to suffer the loss of all things, that he might know Christ and the power of His resurrection.[1] Paul invites us to "copy" him even as he copied Christ.[2]

DANIEL

His faith and convictions influenced the world's greatest empire and withstood the vicious attack of 120 jealous leaders.

ABRAHAM

"He staggered not at the promise of God through unbelief; but was strong in faith, giving glory to God."[3]

INTRODUCE YOUR FAMILY TO THOSE IN SCRIPTURE AND IN HISTORY WHO HAD GREAT FAITH AND GODLY CONVICTIONS

Your sons and daughters are going to imitate others as they grow up. Make sure they imitate the right people.

THE FORMATION OF OUR SELF-IMAGE

The strong desire to be accepted and admired by others will cause a son or daughter to become conscious of whom their parents and friends admire, and for what reasons.

Your son or daughter will usually partially imitate those who are admired. One might be copied in style of dress, another in words or attitudes, and still another in life achievement or skills. For this reason, it is essential that you expose your sons and daughters to the great men and women of faith whom God wants them to imitate.

God gave us their biographies so that they could be examples to us.[4] Their lives will challenge us to achieve the character and life goals that count with God and last for eternity.[5]

HOW TO INTRODUCE GREAT PEOPLE FROM THE BIBLE

A. READ the biographies in Scripture. RELIVE the accounts as if you were there in person. VISUALIZE facial expressions, distances travelled, type of terrain, and surrounding circumstances. Make use of maps and Bible dictionaries.

DAVID: I Samuel 16 - I Kings 2 (David is mentioned more than any other man in the Bible.)

ADAM and NOAH: Genesis 1-12

ABRAHAM, ISAAC, JACOB, and JOSEPH: Genesis 12-50 (God describes the kind of God He is through His dealings with them: "I am the God of Abraham, Isaac, and Jacob.")[6]

MOSES: Exodus 1 - Deuteronomy 34

JOSHUA: Joshua 1-24

B. Select significant experiences in their lives and work out quiz questions for your family at mealtime. Offer a reward to the first one who gives the correct answer.[7]

C. Meditate on the biographies in order to see deeper insights and applications for the situations that you and your family experience. Explain these insights and comparisons whenever it is appropriate.

> "I HAVE MORE UNDERSTANDING THAN ALL MY TEACHERS: FOR THY TESTIMONIES ARE MY MEDITATION."[8]

1. Philippians 3:8-10.
2. I Corinthians 11:1.
3. Romans 4:20.
4. I Corinthians 10:11.
5. Hebrews 11; 12:1.
6. Matthew 22:32.
7. See instructions and illustrations in Character Sketches, Volume II, pp. 15, 16.
8. Psalm 119:99.

HOW TO INTRODUCE GREAT PEOPLE FROM HISTORY

Down through Church history, God has raised up great men and women of faith and Scriptural convictions. Their lives are rich with illustrations and examples for us to follow, especially in learning the cost of true discipleship.

A. Purchase the biographies of those whom God has used to change the course of history. Begin a special bookshelf of great Christians.

B. As you read the biographies, note illustrations of self-acceptance, responding to authority, clear conscience, forgiveness, moral purity, purpose in life, dating standards, and financial principles. Include positive and negative illustrations. Note Godly character qualities. Note special situations and experiences which would illustrate the principles and the character qualities.

C. Learn how to turn interesting illustrations into short accounts that you can relate to your family and friends.

THE THEBIAN LEGION

During the reign of Nero, in the first century, repeated persecutions were brought against Christians. Yet the greater the persecutions, the more the early Church grew.

One day Nero ordered all of his armies to assemble near the city of Gaul. Tens of thousands of soldiers were there. They stood at attention to give a loyalty oath which included killing Christians.

The captain of 6,000 men known as The Thebian Legion replied to this oath by saying, "We will fight and die for Nero in battle, but we will not kill Christians. We ourselves are all Christians."

Nero became infuriated. He ordered their ranks to be decimated. Every tenth man was killed by the sword. The remaining legion still refused. More men were killed until the entire legion was martyred for their faith.

The tens of thousands who watched saw men who had something worth dying for. Soon, thousands became converted, and in A.D. 313 the entire Roman empire adopted the Christian faith.

THE LOLLARDS

All Bibles were outlawed for the common people in England when King Edward III ruled the land. Any Bible that was seen by officials was burned. In spite of this, the people learned more and more of the Bible. Dedicated men, called the Lollards, memorized large portions of Scripture, went into villages, and taught whole groups to memorize the Bible for themselves. The Word could never be taken from them.

WILLIAM CAREY

He said of himself, "I am just an ordinary man. I am a plodder." Through great personal trials, he translated portions of the Bible into over 30 other languages! His life motto was "Attempt great things for God. Expect great things from God."

> # HE THAT WALKETH WITH WISE MEN SHALL BE WISE: BUT A COMPANION OF FOOLS SHALL BE DESTROYED
>
> (Proverbs 13:20)

To help spread the Gospel, John Wycliffe sent out travelling preachers. They were known as Lollards. Some of them were burned because of their faith.

117

SET A DATE   **BE ON TIME**

THE PERSONAL CONFERENCE

God expects every father to meet with each child personally to guide, encourage, and challenge each one to "walk worthy of God."[1]

Your sons and daughters know that you make appointments to see important people. You plan for the meeting and you are on time. You tell them how important they are by doing the same things with them.

QUESTIONS TO REMOVE DOUBTS

1. **What events led up to your becoming a Christian?**

2. **Since becoming a Christian, do you have doubts about your salvation?**

3. **Do you know what is causing the doubts? (Review possible causes.)**

4. **Would you like to get rid of the doubts? (Take proper steps.)**

5. **Since becoming a Christian, has there ever been a time when you totally dedicated your life to God for His will?**

6. **Is there anything that would hinder you from doing that now?**

7. **Follow the salvation prayer on page 120.**

---

1. I Thessalonians 2:11-13.
2. Hebrews 11:6.
3. Hebrews 11:3.
4. Romans 10:17.
5. I Peter 2:2.
6. Romans 10:9-10.
7. Matthew 3:14-15.
8. Romans 12:1-2.
9. I Timothy 1:19.
10. Matthew 6:15.
11. II Peter 1:1-10.
12. Matthew 12:31

BE STRONG IN FAITH!

Faith is a major starting point for success in your own life and for instilling God's ways in your family. "...Without faith it is impossible to please him; for he that cometh to God must believe that he is [that God lives], and that he is a rewarder of them that diligently seek him."[2]

● **KNOW WHAT FAITH IS**

Faith is understanding the ways of God.[3]
Faith is visualizing what God is able to do in the life of a totally dedicated believer.
Faith is discerning what God wants to do in your life and family.

● **KNOW HOW FAITH BEGINS AND GROWS**

Faith is activated by hearing the Word of God.[4]
Faith grows by learning and applying the basic principles of Scripture.[5]

● **BUILD FAITH IN GOD'S WORD**

Confirm Personal Salvation

Never assume that your children are Christians. Find out from them when and where they made a decision to accept and follow Christ. Help them trace any doubts about their salvation to their source and solution.

CAUSES OF DOUBT	STEPS TO REMOVE DOUBTS
Childhood Decision	Pray with them to reaffirm salvation.
Silent Prayer Without Verbal Confession	"O God, I do now reaffirm my faith in Your Son, the Lord Jesus Christ. I confess that He died and rose again for me a sinner. Cleanse me by His blood and make me Your child from this moment forward."[6]
Neglect of Baptism	Arrange for a baptismal service.[7]
Lack of Dedication	Pray together to dedicate life to God.[8]
Need for Restitution	Give direction on clearing conscience.[9]
Secret Bitterness	Teach how to fully forgive.[10]
Lack of Scripture	Challenge to memorize four verses: Romans 10:9-13 I Corinthians 10:13 I John 5:13 I John 1:9
Lack of Growth	Add to faith, character, knowledge...[11]
"Unpardonable Sin"	Explain that this is not a one-time sin, but a continuous rejection of the Holy Spirit's prompting for repentance unto salvation.[12]

For further resource material on salvation, see section 9 in the <u>Basic Seminar Textbook</u> and the Introduction of the <u>Life Notebook</u>.

INSTILL CONFIDENCE IN GOD'S DESIGN

● **BY FAITH WE UNDERSTAND**

In dealing with the fallacies of evolution, we do not need more facts, we need more faith. "Through faith we understand that the worlds were framed by the word of God..."[1]

● **THE INFINITE WISDOM AND PURPOSE OF GOD**

The more we understand about how we are formed in the womb, the more we see how accurate the Word of God really is. God has purpose in the minutest detail of our physical, mental, emotional, and spiritual development.

> If the members of your family reject the way that God made them, they will also tend to reject the Lord and His Word.

● Study the following material and share it during a time with your family.

● **THE ACCURACY AND PRECISENESS OF GOD'S WORD**

PSALM 139:13-16	HEBREW WORD MEANINGS[2]	THE NEWEST MEDICAL RESEARCH[3]
"For thou hast possessed my reins:	*qanah*: erected, created	CELL: Chromosome DNA Ladder The "fence" of "inner intelligence" which God "erected."
"thou hast covered me in my mother's womb.	*sakak*: entwined, fenced in	
"I will praise thee; for I am fearfully	*Yare*: to revere, to be afraid of misusing	
"and wonderfully made:	*palah*: to distinguish	All the forms and functions of our body are determined by messages within the DNA molecules. These DNA molecules are structured like a fence or a ladder. Just before the cell divides, the twisted fence structure of the DNA divides down the middle. Each side becomes a duplicate of the original one.
"marvelous are thy works; and that my soul knoweth right well.	*pala*: to separate, to differentiate	
"My substance was not hid from thee, when I was	*otsem*: from *atsam*: to bind fast, power, body	
"made in secret, and	*cithrah* from *cthar*: to hide, to conceal, to keep secret	Chromosome
"curiously wrought in the	*raqam*: to variegate color, to diversify, to give variety	Divided DNA Ladder
"lowest parts of the earth.	*serets*: earth, the elements of man are identical to those in dust	
"Thine eyes did see my substance, yet being unperfect;	*golem*, from *galam*: to wrap together, unformed mass; i.e., embryo	
"and in thy book all my members	*siphrah*, from *sepher*: to record, to inscribe, to enynerate	Each cell contains three feet of DNA ladders. If all the DNA cells in an adult man were put end to end, the ladders would extend to the sun and back over three and a half times. The total length would be ten million miles. Every minute, about three billion cells in our body die and about three billion new cells are born to replace them.
"were written, which in continuance	*kathab*: to engrave, to prescribe and describe	
"were fashioned, when as yet there was none of them."	*yatsar*: to determine,　to mold into a form	

1. Hebrews 11:3.　　2. Strong's Exhaustive Concordance, Hebrew Dictionary of the Bible.
3. The World Book Encyclopedia, Field Enterprises Educational Corporation, Vol. 3, "Cell," p. 250; The Science Library, Time Incorporated, New York, "The Cell," Pfeiffer, pp. 68-74.

☐ Study page 118.
☐ Complete Application No. 22.
☐ Define Quality No. 8 (page 6).

QUESTION No. 22

How can I remove doubts which hinder the assurance of salvation?

ANSWER:

You can remove doubts which hinder your assurance of salvation by understanding the basic causes which prompt doubts and by reaffirming the prayer of salvation.

QUIZ No. 22   **CAN YOU HELP A PERSON REMOVE DOUBTS?**
(Match the best step of action with each cause.)

1. Childhood Decision: "I was too young."

   A. ☐ **Humble yourself before God.**
   "...Whosoever shall confess me before men, him shall the Son of man also confess before the angels of God" (Luke 12:8).

2. Silent Prayer: "I prayed to myself."

   B. ☐ **Clear up past offenses. Then reaffirm salvation.**
   "...Holding faith, and a good conscience; which some having put away...have made shipwreck [of their faith]" (I Timothy 1:18-19).

3. Point of Pride: "I refuse to confess Christ."

   C. ☐ **Confess your sin and ask God for His grace.**
   "For it is God which worketh in you both to will and to do of his good pleasure" (Philippians 2:13).

4. Need for Restitution: "I've offended many."

   D. ☐ **Obey the Lord in baptism.**
   "...It becometh us to fulfill all righteousness...And Jesus, when he was baptized, went up straightway out of the water..." (Matthew 3:15-16).

5. Bitterness: "I'll never forgive a certain person."

   E. ☐ **Realize that the unpardonable sin is not a one-time act, but a continuous rejection of the Holy Spirit's conviction to become a Christian.**
   "...Christ Jesus came into the world to save sinners; of whom I [Paul] am chief" (I Timothy 1:15).
   "...I...compelled them to blaspheme..." (Acts 26:11).

6. Neglect of Baptism: "I've never been baptized."

   F. ☐ **Pray aloud with someone.**
   "For with the heart man believeth unto righteousness; and with the mouth confession is made unto salvation" (Romans 10:10).

7. Secret Sins: "I don't want to give something up."

   G. ☐ **Thank God for this clear evidence of salvation.**
   "...I will send him [the Holy Spirit] unto you. And when he is come, he will reprove...of sin, and of righteousness, and of judgment" (John 16:7-8).

8. Unpardonable Sin: "I've blasphemed the Holy Spirit."

   H. ☐ **Pray again to reaffirm your childhood decision.**
   "...Suffer little children to come unto me, and forbid them not: for of such is the kingdom of God" (Luke 18:16).

9. Greater Conviction: "I feel like a greater sinner now."

   I. ☐ **Fully forgive and reaffirm your salvation.**
   "...If ye forgive not men their trespasses, neither will your Father forgive your trespasses" (Matthew 6:15).

PROVIDE COPIES FOR YOUR FAMILY.

APPLICATION No. 22

1. Purpose to help each one in your family to remove any doubts about salvation.

Thank You, Lord, for an inheritance incorruptible and undefiled, that does not fade away, reserved in heaven for us who are kept by Your power through faith unto salvation....[1]

2. Ask each one in your family personally what events led up to his or her salvation, whether there have been any doubts about salvation since then, and, if so, would he or she like to remove the doubts.

3. Go over the plan of salvation with any who have doubts about salvation.

☐ God loves each one of us.
"For God so loved the world, that he gave his only begotten Son, that whosoever believeth on him should not perish, but have everlasting life" (John 3:16).

☐ Each one of us has sinned.
"For all have sinned, and come short of the glory of God" (Romans 3:23).

☐ No sin can enter heaven.
"For the wages of sin is death; but the gift of God is eternal life through Jesus Christ our Lord" (Romans 8:23).

☐ Jesus died to pay the full penalty for all of our sin.
"But God commendeth his love toward us, in that, while we were yet sinners, Christ died for us" (Romans 5:8).

☐ God gives His eternal salvation to all who will put their full trust in Christ's death and resurrection.
"For by grace are ye saved through faith; and that not of yourselves: it is the gift of God. Not of works, lest any man should boast" (Ephesians 2:8-9).

"That if thou shalt confess with thy mouth the Lord Jesus, and shalt believe in thine heart that God hath raised him from the dead, thou shalt be saved" (Romans 10:9).

4. Offer to lead in a prayer to confirm salvation. It is important to pray out loud with the person. You might suggest that the person pray one phrase at a time after you.

> **PRAYER TO GAIN ASSURANCE OF SALVATION:**
>
> *Heavenly Father, thank You for loving me and sending Your own Son to die for all my sin. Thank You for raising Him up from the dead. Right now, I do confess that I am a sinner. I ask You to cleanse me through the shed blood of the Lord Jesus Christ. Thank You for now receiving me as Your child and for giving to me eternal life.*

5. After the person prays, ask, "Do you think God heard your prayer? What gives us the assurance that He did hear your prayer?" (Answer: The Word of God, not our emotions.)

6. Explain six evidences of salvation.

☐ A new love for God's Word. (Begin a Bible reading program.)
☐ A new awareness of right and wrong. (You may feel like a greater sinner after salvation because God's Spirit is in you convicting of sins which displease God.)
☐ A desire to become like Christ. (Christ in you the hope of glory.)
☐ A desire to win your friends to Christ. (Be loving and tactful.)
☐ Social pressure from those who are not Christians.
☐ A love for other Christians. (Become active in a Bible-believing church.)

7. Give the quiz on removing doubts.
ANSWERS TO QUIZ:

1. H	4. B	7. C
2. F	5. I	8. E
3. A	6. D	9. G

1. Personalization of I Peter 1:4-5.

TWENTY-THIRD WEEK:

☐ Study pages 115-117.
☐ Complete Application No. 23.
☐ Identify Quality No. 8 (page 6).

QUESTION No. 23
How can I motivate my family to build Godly character into their lives?

ANSWER:

The first step in building Godly character qualities in the lives of your family is to identify and define these character qualities. You can then work with your wife and your family in emphasizing one character quality each week. The goal of building Godly character into your life and family has infinite possibilities.

QUIZ No. 23   CAN YOU IDENTIFY CHARACTER QUALITIES?
(Match the "operational definition" with each quality.)

QUALITIES		OPERATIONAL DEFINITIONS
1. Attentiveness	A. ☐	Learning how to wait to fulfill personal goals. Increasing the time you can wait between achievement and reward. Learning to accept difficult situations as from God without giving Him a deadline to remove them.
2. Obedience	B. ☐	Learning to demonstrate Christ's love toward an offender. Understanding the motives and conflicts of an offender. Remembering how much God has forgiven us. Learning to see spiritual value in the hurts God allows through other people.
3. Neatness	C. ☐	Learning to be a reliable messenger. Gaining approval of others without misrepresenting the facts. Facing the consequences of a mistake.
4. Reverence	D. ☐	Learning to see life from God's perspective. Recognizing a cause and effect relationship in life. Tracing conflicts to their root causes. Learning how to apply principles of life in daily situations. Discerning false philosophies and natural inclinations and rejecting them.
5. Forgiveness	E. ☐	Learning to arrange my schedule around the appointments that are made. Showing esteem for other people and their time by not keeping them waiting.
6. Gratefulness	F. ☐	Learning to organize and care for personal possessions. Giving attention to personal grooming. Learning to write legibly. Learning cleanliness.
7. Truthfulness	G. ☐	Adopting as your own the wishes and goals of those you are serving. Learning to stand by those you are serving when conflicting pressures increase.
8. Patience	H. ☐	Learning to quickly identify and obey the initial promptings of the Holy Spirit. Bringing my thoughts, words, and actions under the control of the Holy Spirit.
9. Punctuality	I. ☐	Learning the importance of limitations and the meaning of the word "no." Responding to the wishes of God, parents, and others in authority. Yielding the right to have the final decision.
10. Loyalty	J. ☐	Learning to recognize the benefits which God and others have provided. Looking for appropriate ways to express genuine appreciation. Learning to give all expectations to God.
11. Wisdom	K. ☐	Learning to respect the possessions and property of others. Recognizing how God works through those in authority. Giving proper honor to people in positions of authority and learning how God works through them to give protection and build character. Learning to care for our body as the temple of the Holy Spirit.
12. Self-Control	L. ☐	Learning the wishes of parents through facial expressions, words, and tone of voice. Listening to conscience, God's Word, and the promptings of the Holy Spirit to learn God's moral standards and will.

APPLICATION No. 23

1. Purpose to motivate your family to build Godly character qualities into their lives.

> *"My little children, of whom I travail in birth again until Christ be formed in you."*[1]

2. Commit yourself to making your wife "radiant with God's Word."[2]

One wife reported: "It is difficult to share the joy I experienced as my husband pursued this project. It became a turning point for us in our relationship and in our home.

"He carried a little notebook, and he would give me Scripture verses to meet all kinds of daily situations. There were times when I knew that he spent hours looking up Scripture and topics that would benefit me. There were other times when he would get up earlier just to pray for me and the children in private before we would have our time together.

"As my husband became more sensitive to me as a woman and for my outreach to others, God restored a deep desire in me to please him. I began to desire all the qualities which would help me meet his needs."[3]

DEEPEN MARRIAGE COMMUNICATION THROUGH CHARACTER BUILDING

☐ Select one of the character qualities on the previous page. During the week work individually on a study of that quality. Find illustrations of it in the lives of men and women in the Bible. See consequences when it was violated, or benefits when it was demonstrated.

☐ During the second week, do all that you can to incorporate this quality into your life and home. Discover strengths and weaknesses in yourself, your home, your marriage, and in your children. Observe ways that you can design projects which will help to build the quality.

☐ In the second meeting with your wife, write out and discuss the following statements. Then pray together. Confess your needs, and commit yourselves to developing this quality in your lives and family.

1. **Specific ways in which you demonstrated** *(attentiveness)* .
2. **Specific ways in which you failed to demonstrate** *(attentiveness)* .
3. **My inward emotions when you demonstrate** *(attentiveness)* .
4. **My emotions when you fail to demonstrate** *(attentiveness)* .
5. **My outward response when you demonstrate** *(attentiveness)* .
6. **My response when you fail to demonstrate** *(attentiveness)* .
7. **What God is teaching me when you demonstrate** *(attentiveness)* .
8. **What God is teaching me when you fail to demonstrate** *(attentiveness)* .

---

3. Give your family the quiz on character qualities.

☐ Jesus Christ was the personification of all Godly character. The more we learn about Godly character, the more we learn about Christ.

☐ **QUIZ ANSWERS:**

1. L	4. K	7. C	10. G
2. I	5. B	8. A	11. D
3. F	6. J	9. E	12. H

1. Galatians 4:19.
2. Ephesians 5:25-26.
3. Used by permission.

QUESTION No. 24

How can I help a member of my family accept physical and family defects?

ANSWER:

You can help a member of your family accept physical and family defects by teaching him or her how to turn that defect into a "mark of ownership," and to see how God is using it to build Godly character qualities in his or her life.

WHAT ARE YOUR "MARKS OF OWNERSHIP"?

☐ Paul said: "...I bear in my body the marks of the Lord Jesus."[1] The Greek word for "marks" is *"stigma."* It means a mark put for recognition of ownership[2] (a brand).

☐ What "marks" (unchangeable physical or family features) are a "stigma" to you? These are marks of ownership. Your "marks" are the features you would like to change about your...

height	ears	skin blemishes	upbringing
hair	teeth	mind abilities	scars
face	feet	heritage	deformities
eyes	skin color	family	handicaps
nose	bone structure	parents	infirmities

QUIZ No. 24

WHO IN SCRIPTURE HAD "MARKS OF OWNERSHIP"?
(Match the person with the "mark of ownership.")

1. Who sat at the table of a king because of a physical handicap?

2. Who attracted national attention because of a physical uniqueness, especially in the hands and the feet?

3. Who was promised extra strength because of a physical affliction?

4. Who was given power with God in exchange for a physical limitation?

5. Who was given a double portion of miraculous power but had a physical feature which caused some to mock him?

6. Who was rejected because of physical unattractiveness but was blessed of God because of it?

7. Who was disinherited because of being born of a harlot but was used of God to become a national hero?

A. ☐ PAUL
   II Corinthians 12:9

B. ☐ JACOB
   Genesis 32:32

C. ☐ LEAH
   Genesis 29:17, 31

D. ☐ THE GIANT'S SON
   II Samuel 21:20

E. ☐ JEPHTHAH
   Judges 11:3

F. ☐ ELISHA
   II Kings 2:23

G. ☐ MEPHIBOSHETH
   II Samuel 9:6-13

1. Galatians 6:17.
2. Strong's Exhaustive Concordance, Greek Dictionary of the New Testament, p. 67, No. 4742.

APPLICATION No. 24

1. Purpose to help each member in your family accept physical and family defects.

I will praise You, for I am fearfully and wonderfully made: marvelous are Your works, and that my soul knoweth right well.[1]

2. Begin by applying the principle of self-acceptance to your marriage.

☐ Realize that God made you and your wife with loving care and wise design.

☐ Thank God for unchangeable physical and family features in you and your wife as God's special "marks of ownership."

☐ Accept unchangeable physical features as God's outward frame for the inward character of Christ, which He wants you and your wife to develop.

☐ Realize that God will use the weaknesses of each one of you to perfect the character of Christ in you.

☐ Work on any changeable features in order to provide the best frame for Christ's character within you.

3. Present the meaning of "marks" and the quiz on the opposite page.

QUIZ ANSWERS:

1. (G) Mephibosheth was lame in both feet.

2. (D) The giant's son had twelve fingers and twelve toes.

3. (A) Paul was given a "thorn in the flesh."

4. (B) Jacob limped after the angel shrank the sinew of his thigh.

5. (F) Elisha was mocked by children for being bald headed.

6. (C) Leah was given children by God because Jacob hated her.

7. (E) Jephthah was rejected by his half brothers because he was an "illegitimate" son.

4. Begin to visualize how "marks of ownership" can become "thorns of glory."[2] Think through how these "thorns" can develop the following character qualities:

Truthfulness	Diligence	Tolerance
Virtue	Thoroughness	Cautiousness
Self-Control	Dependability	Gratefulness
Contentment	Confidence	Neatness
Fairness	Patience	Initiative
Persuasiveness	Wisdom	Responsibility
Boldness	Discernment	Courage
Alertness	Discretion	Decisiveness
Hospitality	Faith	Determination
Joyfulness	Forgiveness	Loyalty
Generosity	Creativity	Sensitivity
Flexibility	Enthusiasm	Compassion
Availability	Resourcefulness	Obedience
Endurance	Thriftiness	Gentleness
Accuracy	Sincerity	Politeness
Reverence	Punctuality	Meekness
		Attentiveness

1. Personalization of Psalm 139:14.
2. II Corinthians 12:6-9.

TWENTY-FIFTH WEEK:

- ☐ Study pages 112-114.
- ☐ Complete Application No. 25.
- ☐ Define Quality No. 9 (page 6).

QUESTION No. 25

What if my family asks me questions about the Christian life which I do not know how to answer?

ANSWER:

If your family asks a question about the Christian life for which you have no answer, be a learner with them and search for the answer. A wise father is not a man who has all the answers, but one who will take necessary time and effort to find the right answers. As you bring a question to God's Word, review in your mind the basic principles of Scripture, the testimonies of God's dealings with people, the ways of God (birth, death, and fulfillment of a vision), and the precise instructions of Proverbs. Then ask God for wisdom.[1]

QUIZ No. 25   DO YOU KNOW HOW GOD GIVES WISDOM FROM HIS WORD?
(Match the following questions with the most appropriate answers on the right.)

1. Before I was a Christian, I stole tools from a neighbor. Do I have to take them back now?
2. Isn't it all right to wish that some day he will get the punishment he deserves?
3. Next year I'll be 18. Will I be old enough then to be on my own?
4. Many times I look in the mirror and wonder why I could not have been more attractive.
5. What is wrong with going out once in a while and having a little "fun"?
6. I try to get along with my father, but he is really a strange person.
7. The rock band has come back with a better offer. Should I ask God once more if I should join?
8. Is it right for a city to make laws against moral perversion? Don't perverted people only hurt themselves?
9. My friends are going to visit a witch. Could I go along just to see what happens?
10. My husband divorced me and my son really needs a father image. Shouldn't I remarry?
11. I know that God has called me into Christian work. Why should I let my wife stand in the way?
12. I worked as hard as I could for that church. Why did they treat me the way they did?
13. My friend asked me to co-sign a loan he is getting. What should I tell him?
14. What should I do if I can't pay my bills and tithe at the same time?
15. Isn't it all right to earn more bank interest by holding off payment of my bills?

A. ☐ KING SAUL
B. ☐ DO NOT BE SURETY
C. ☐ BALAAM
D. ☐ SODOM
E. ☐ PAY PROMPTLY
F. ☐ SELF-ACCEPTANCE
G. ☐ TITHE FIRST
H. ☐ DEATH OF VISION
I. ☐ CLEAR CONSCIENCE
J. ☐ MORAL FREEDOM
K. ☐ FORGIVENESS
L. ☐ MICHAL
M. ☐ CHAIN OF COMMAND
N. ☐ TIMOTHY'S MOTHER
O. ☐ CALLING TO SUFFER

PROVIDE COPIES FOR YOUR FAMILY. | WAYS OF GOD | TESTIMONIES OF SCRIPTURE | BASIC PRINCIPLES | PROVERBS

1. James 1:5.

126

APPLICATION No. 25

1. Purpose to search out the answers to questions which your family has about the Christian life.

> *"Open thou mine eyes, that I may behold wondrous things out of thy law."*[1]

2. Plan special times alone with your wife for intimate conversation. Encourage her to share with you her fears and wishes.

3. Encourage the members of your family to share their questions with you.

☐ Play "The Answer Game" with your younger children. Just before bedtime, most children enjoy finding reasons to stay up longer. Tell them that when they are ready for bed, you will give each one an opportunity to ask any question they want about the Bible, about God, or about how to live as a Christian. You will give them the best answer that you know. If you do not know the answer immediately, you will do all you can to find the answer for them.

☐ Encourage your older sons and daughters to share their questions with you by asking them questions:

- What are the biggest hindrances that you find to getting into God's Word every day?
- What do you think the attitudes of your teachers are regarding the authority and accuracy of the Bible?
- What is your favorite verse or person in the Bible and why?
- What is the most difficult question that you have about the Bible or the Christian life?

☐ Use every resource that you can in finding God's answers.

- Ask God for His wisdom as Solomon did.[2]
- Use a concordance to look up related topics and illustrations.
- Draw upon the lessons which God has already taught you.
- Become acquainted with the writings of great Christians.
- Ask your spiritual leaders for further insights and resource material.

4. Give your family the quiz on getting wisdom (opposite page).

1. (I) God gives power to Christians to clear their consciences (I Timothy 1:18-19).

2. (K) To forgive is to want their best (Matthew 5:44).

3. (M) We must always be under the counsel of our parents (Proverbs 22:22).

4. (F) The inward beauty of Christ will be seen outwardly (Ecclesiastes 8:1).

5. (J) The pleasures of sin last only for a season (Hebrews 11:25).

6. (L) Michal's response to her father was transferred to David (I Samuel 18:21; I Corinthians 15:29).

7. (C) Never ask God twice for what He has told you once is wrong (Numbers 22-24; 31:8; Jude 11).

8. (D) The burning lust of perversion is like a fire that cannot be contained. It destroys cities (Genesis 19; Jude 7).

9. (A) King Saul lost his life for going to a witch (I Samuel 28).

10. (N) Timothy did not have a "father image" in his family. His mother and grandmother directed him to Paul (II Timothy 1:5).

11. (H) God calls us, then he teaches us (in His classroom), then he sends us (Matthew 20:16).

12. (O) God purifies our motives in suffering (I Peter 4:12).

13. (B) Never co-sign a note (Proverbs 6:1-5).

14. (G) Give to God first, then He will bless (Proverbs 3:9).

15. (E) Do not postpone paying bills (Proverbs 3:28).

1. Psalm 119:18.
2. I Kings 3:9-14.

QUESTION No. 26

What should I do if someone in my family rejects the Word of God and lives in rebellion?

ANSWER:

If someone in your family rejects the Word of God and lives in rebellion, you should use this situation as a motivation to examine your own life, then discern the real needs in the life of that person. Based on this examination, "bind" Satan through prayer, and cast down false reasonings which Satan has built in the mind of the individual.[1]

THE POWER OF "BINDING" SATAN AND BUILDING A "WALL OF PROTECTION"

The wife of a young minister left him and began living with the owner of a night club. The minister learned about the "hedge." He began to pray that God would put such a strong hedge around his unfaithful wife that anyone near her would be uncomfortable, and that she would lose favor with her lovers. The night after he began praying this way, God began to act.

The customers would only stay for a few minutes and then unexplainably excuse themselves and leave. The next night the same thing happened and even fewer men bothered to notice her at all. Finally, three nights later the boss came over and demanded that she get out. When she reminded him about their marriage plans, he only laughed and ordered her to leave.

In shame and confusion, she called her husband at 2:30 a.m. She wept out her story, then said, "I have no place to go!" Her husband told her that she could come home. She sobbed, "You mean you would take me back after all that I've done against you?" The husband replied, "Not only will I take you back, but I'll come and get you now."

It was only one week after the husband prayed in this manner that his wife was back home.

READ THIS TO YOUR FAMILY.

QUIZ No. 26   WHO PROTECTED OTHERS THROUGH PRAYER?
(Match the questions with the proper person on the right.)

1. Who protected a relative from the fires of God's wrath and almost succeeded in protecting a city as well?

2. Who protected his family through prayer so that Satan had to get special permission from God in order to bring any harm to them?

3. Who protected a follower through intercessory prayer from being "sifted as wheat by Satan"?

4. Who protected a man from the wrath of a cruel king by praying for him?

5. Who protected thousands from God's judgment of poisonous snakes by praying for them?

6. Who "prayed to God always" and as a result saw God bring salvation to his whole family?

A. ☐ CORNELIUS
Acts 10

B. ☐ JESUS CHRIST
Luke 22:31

C. ☐ EARLY CHRISTIANS
Acts 12

D. ☐ MOSES
Numbers 21:7

E. ☐ ABRAHAM
Genesis 18-19

F. ☐ JOB
Job 1

PRAYER TO "BIND" SATAN AND BUILD A "HEDGE":

"Heavenly Father, as the spiritual leader in my family, I purpose to resist the Devil in my own life. I ask You, in the name and through the blood of the Lord Jesus Christ, to bind Satan in the lives of my family. Build around their minds, wills, and emotions a wall of protection. Forbid Satan from giving any further aid or benefit to any false reasonings in their minds. Require Satan to gain permission from You for any further activity in their lives. Thank You for Your victory through Christ."

Based on II Corinthians 10:4-5; John 17:15.

1. II Corinthians 10:4-5.
The above illustration is used by permission.

APPLICATION No. 26

1. Purpose to build a spiritual "wall of protection" around each member of your family.

Lord, You "sought for a man...that should make up the hedge, and stand in the gap before" You, that You "should not destroy..." but you found none.[1]

2. Realize that God has given you special spiritual authority because you are responsible for the spiritual welfare of your family. You are the "strong man" of your household. Satan is the "strong man" of his household.

You must be "one that ruleth well his own house, having his children in subjection with all gravity."[2]

"No man can enter into a strong man's house and spoil his goods, except he will first bind the strong man; and then he will spoil his house."[3]

3. Be aware that Satan can "bind" you by sinful habits. You can "bind" Satan through the righteousness of Christ and by His name and His blood. Christ has already shown Himself "stronger" than the strong man (Satan).[4]

4. As you "bind" Satan in the lives of members of your family, you are building a "hedge" or a "spiritual wall of protection" around them. Then you can tear down the false reasonings which Satan has constructed in their minds against the truth of God's Word.

5. Realize that there are spiritual prerequisites for this protective prayer.

An example of building a wall of protection around the family is given from the life of Job. Three times God emphasized the qualities which allowed Him to answer Job's prayer.[5]

1. He was **PERFECT** *(tam)*: For us, this involves being "complete" in Christ's righteousness, and "undefiled" with moral impurity.
2. He was **UPRIGHT** *(yashar)*: To be fair and just in all dealings. This requires a clear conscience.
3. He **FEARED** God *(yare)*: To regard every thought, word, attitude, or act with worshipful respect for God's reputation.
4. He **HATED** evil *(suwr)*: To go out of your way to avoid evil at any cost.

SELF-EXAMINATION QUESTIONS:

1. Have I neglected daily prayer for this person? (I Samuel 12:23)
2. Have I offended this person and never asked forgiveness? (I Peter 3:16)
3. Have I failed to be alert to their spiritual dangers? (I Corinthians 16:13-14)
4. Did I fail to give lasting answers to impure habits? (Ephesians 6:4)
5. Did I fail to make the Christian life challenging? (Hebrews 10:24)

6. Give the quiz on prayer.

QUIZ ANSWERS:

1. E	3. B	5. D
2. F	4. C	6. A

1. A personalization of Ezekiel 22:30.
2. I Timothy 3:4.
3. Mark 3:27.
4. Luke 11:22; Ephesians 1:20-21.
5. Job 1:1, 8; 2:3.

☐ Review pages 77-79.
☐ Complete Application No. 27.
☐ Develop Quality No. 9 (page 6).

QUESTION No. 27

What counsel should I give my sons and daughters if they are ever required to study "humanistic" philosophies, or a false religion?

ANSWER:

Do you know the danger of studying false philosophies? They appeal to the mind with deceptive logic, and even if their error is detected and rejected, they remain in the mind to distract from discovering the rich, deep truths of God's Word. It is for this reason that Scripture commands us to discern error with our (God's) Spirit and reject it, rather than trying to study error with our minds and attempt to come to an "intellectual conclusion."

Based on this danger, reject any course or book which majors on the details of humanistic philosophies or false religions. Also, do not take any courses on religion from a teacher who rejects the inspiration of Scripture.

HOW TWO STUDENTS BECAME WISER THAN THEIR TEACHERS[1]

"We are twins attending a Christian college, majoring in math. This past summer we had to attend another college in order to graduate. The psychology teacher made it clear to us that she thought there was no God. She proceeded to talk about sex whenever she could. To her, there is no right or wrong, no absolutes. She exhibited a real disdain for the law and a contempt for parents. Her idols are B. F. Skinner and Aldous Huxley.

"She showed us a movie interview with Huxley. He was gaunt, extremely nervous, hollow-eyed and unable to answer questions in a lucid manner. He was pathetic, a wretched man with no peace or meaning to his life. The next movie she showed was filthy. We left the room. A third movie depicted a plural marriage. It would be impossible to express how utterly ugly it was. We both felt such a deep hurt and grief, and, again, we left the room.

"Through all this, Dad and Mom were really praying for us. It was SO GOOD to be under Dad's umbrella of protection. Many times we thought about students who were separated from their parents and attending a school like this. How could those parents possibly know what their son or daughter was really going through? We concluded that God did not intend young folks to go to courses like this. Parents would be shocked to know what is being taught in classrooms today.

"The next class was philosophy. From the outset, the professor made it emphatically clear that ALL truth comes from reason—from man's own mind. He began with Socrates, explaining what he thought was his tremendous wisdom. But we discovered on our own that Socrates admitted that he talked to a demon from time to time. He also consulted the Oracle of Delphi, informing him that he was the wisest man on earth. He also had a homosexual relationship with Plato, his young protege. So we wrote our essay which infuriated the professor. We ended the essay with, 'So it is easy to see that a man's morality dictates his philosophy.'

"We explained that we were not as interested in the fact that these philosophers did not believe in God as much as why they did not believe in God. We would go into their early lives and clearly point out root problems. In each case, there was a decision to be morally impure even though in just about every case there was some kind of Christian background. Soon after the decision to become immoral came the turning away from God which then led to atheism. Finally, they were forced to choose a philosophy that would fit their life style.

"Nietzsche had syphilis at age 22. He gave up his professorship at 35 because of syphilis-related health problems and was totally insane at age 46. His writings were the result of a diseased mind as was his statement that God is dead. What a price to pay for impurity.

"Marx had an immoral relationship at an extremely early age, became estranged from his parents, was influenced and befriended by an older man—a philosopher, left home to go to school, reinforced his earlier decision regarding moral impurity, became an atheist and developed his own philosophy. He and his wife and children lived in abject poverty because he would not work. He coveted material things and power. He and Engels planned to be co-dictators and rule the world together. He was filled with hate for all, especially this proletariat. He had illegitimate children. Two of his daughters committed suicide.

"We proved, beyond any measure of doubt, that these philosophers all violated certain principles, and therefore, suffered specific results in their lives. We would never have thought to question the professor's opinions, nor would we have thought to research each philosopher's life if we had not learned at the Seminar that a man's morality dictates his philosophy."

READ THIS TO YOUR FAMILY.

1. Used by permission.

APPLICATION No. 27

1. Purpose to protect your wife, sons, and daughters from the destructiveness of false philosophies and false religions.

We will guard our heart, with all diligence, for out of it are the issues of life.[1]

2. Ask your family what they would do if they were in a school that required them to read a Godless philosophy book.

☐ Explain why we must discern error with our Spirit (opposite page).

☐ Give the Scripture which commands Christians to avoid false philosophies.

● "Beware lest any man spoil you through philosophy and vain deceit, after the tradition of men, after the rudiments of the world, and not after Christ" (Colossians 2:8).
● "But shun profane and vain babblings: for they will increase unto more ungodliness. And their word will eat as doth a canker [gangrene]..." (II Timothy 2:16–17).
● "But avoid foolish questions...for they are unprofitable and vain. A man that is an heretick after the first and second admonition reject; knowing that he that is such is subverted, and sinneth, being condemned of himself" (Titus 3:9-11).
● "But foolish and unlearned questions avoid, knowing that they do gender strifes. And the servant of the Lord must not strive..." (II Timothy 2:23-24).
● "This know also, that in the last days perilous times shall come. For men shall be lovers of their own selves, covetous, boasters, proud, blasphemers...having a form of godliness, but denying the power thereof: from such turn away" (II Timothy 3:1-5).
● "Now I beseech you, brethren, mark them which cause divisions and offenses contrary to the doctrine which ye have learned; and avoid them" (Romans 16:17).
● "...I would have you wise unto that which is good, and simple concerning evil" (Romans 16:17).
● "Cease, my son, to hear the instruction that causeth to err from the words of knowledge" (Proverbs 19:27).
● "Go from the presence of a foolish man, when thou perceivest not in him the lips of knowledge" (Proverbs 14:7).

3. Discuss with your family the sources through which false philosophies are being taught today.

☐ Television   ☐ Public schools
☐ Advertising   ☐ False religions
☐ Secular magazines   ☐ "Religious" books
☐ Newspapers

4. Ask each one in your family to detect at least one illustration of a false philosophy and share it during the next mealtime. The purpose of this is to expose unscriptural ideas and cleanse them from the mind.

● Man did not evolve from lower forms of life.
● Wise guidance for daily decisions does not come by the stars.
● Reading books by false cults is not wise or necessary.
● Forming close friendships with those who reject God's Word will not benefit you or your family.
● Government programs are not going to solve man's basic needs.
● False interpretations of the Bible do not come as a result of scholarship, but as a result of immorality.
● Having books and magazines of false teaching in your library is not a sign of scholarship.

1. Personalization of Proverbs 4:23.

WHAT WAS THE SECRET OF HIS WISDOM?

When Stephen was called before the council to answer false charges, his face became as "the face of an angel,"[1] and when he spoke, no one was "...able to resist the wisdom and the spirit by which he spake."[2] What was the secret of such wisdom?

Stephen was filled with God's Word and was mighty in God's Spirit. He concentrated on the "wisdom that is from above,"[3] not on the wisdom of this world. The qualities of God's wisdom are listed in James 3:17-18.

The wisdom that is from above is first pure, then peaceable, gentle, approachable, full of kindly thoughts and tolerant actions, without favoritism, and without hypocrisy.

1. Acts 6:15.
2. Acts 6:10.
3. James 3:17.

5 BE KIND AND LOVING IN ALL THAT YOU DO!

☐   If a man tries to establish and maintain God's principles in his family and fails to do it in kindness and love, he will cause his wife to react to him and his convictions, and he will provoke his children to wrath.

☐   The command to be kind and loving is a final test of whether a man has fully built God's principles and standards into his own life. A man is usually impatient with others in the very area in which he is failing.

☐   When a member of a man's family resists or rejects his standards or convictions, he is able to learn and demonstrate the kind of love for them that God has for us, even when we rejected Him.

☐   What does it mean to be kind and loving in all that you do? It means to:

- Be committed to the success of each family member.
- Earn the right to be heard—do not demand it.
- Demonstrate a servant's heart and a learner's spirit.
- Give whatever time and energy is necessary.
- Learn to see situations from your family's viewpoint.
- Find out what offends your family and correct it.
- Always watch for pride and conquer it.
- Refuse to be angry or disappointed when your family fails.

QUESTIONS FOR PERSONAL APPLICATION

The following questions are amplified throughout this section and specifically answered on pages 140-145.

28 HOW CAN I LEARN TO BE GENTLE IN THE WAY I TREAT MY WIFE AND FAMILY?

29 HOW CAN I TEACH MY FAMILY TO BE GRATEFUL FOR ALL THE THINGS THAT I DO FOR THEM?

30 HOW CAN I LEARN TO HAVE GENUINE LOVE FOR EACH ONE IN MY FAMILY?

5

BE KIND AND LOVING IN ALL YOU DO!

This is the most important of all five commands. "...Above all things have fervent love...."[1] "...The greatest of these is love."[2]

Many well-meaning fathers have resolved to be the spiritual leaders in their homes, and they have been totally dedicated. They have been consistent, but they have failed because they were not kind and loving.

REALIZE WHY IT IS DIFFICULT FOR MEN TO BE KIND AND LOVING HUSBANDS AND FATHERS

When Adam sinned, the loving leadership of the husband was corrupted, as well as the willing submission of the wife. Since that time, it has been natural for a man to cherish secret desires for unquestioned power and authority, rather than for a loving giving of himself to those whom he is leading.

Satan uses this secret motivation as his basis to plant destructive, harsh, prideful suggestions in the mind of a man. Satan will plant the suggestion to be firm when the man should be lenient, and lenient when he should be firm. Satan will suggest to a man that he demand obedience when he should appeal, and to be severe or sulky when his authority is challenged.

The great problem with these Satanic suggestions is that they will usually not be recognized by the man as having come from Satan. He will think they are his own ideas, because they are exactly what he wants to do. "...Every man is tempted when he is drawn away of his own lust...."[3] In this case, it is a lust for personal power and unchallenged authority. As a man, you must recognize this secret motivation, confess it as sin, and be on guard for Satan's destructive suggestions.

LEARN HOW TO BE KIND AND LOVING IN YOUR LEADERSHIP RESPONSIBILITIES

There are very precise skills that you can learn and steps that you can take in order to demonstrate to your family the kind of leadership which Christ had for the Church when He loved it and gave Himself for it.[4]

DAVID

When Shimei, David's enemy, threw stones at him and cursed him, one of David's generals asked permission to remove Shimei's head. David did not allow the execution because he saw the spiritual significance behind the irritation and recognized that God was speaking to him through it.[5]

USE THE IRRITATIONS OF OTHERS AS SIGNALS FOR SELF-EXAMINATION

One of the reasons that we get so irritated with the faults of others is that we have similar faults in ourselves that we have not yet conquered. If we would have conquered them, we would be sympathetic to the struggles the other person is going through and eager to share the steps of victory. "...Thou that judgest doest the same things."[6] "For with what judgment ye judge, ye shall be judged...."[7]

---

1. I Peter 4:8.
2. I Corinthians 13:13.
3. James 1:14.
4. Ephesians 5:25.

5. II Samuel 19:16-23.
6. Romans 2:1.
7. Matthew 7:2.

IF YOU WANT TO BE AN EFFECTIVE SPIRITUAL LEADER, YOU MUST HAVE THESE SEVEN SKILLS

1. YOU MUST BE IN A CONTINUAL STATE OF GRATEFULNESS TO THE LORD

- A father can be sure that if he fails to express genuine gratefulness to those in his own family for the efforts they make (large or small) to please him, they will cease to make the effort.

- A further benefit of a father's gratefulness is that it will promote an atmosphere of gratefulness within the home. His family will learn how to express their gratefulness as they see him doing it.

- A basic aspect of gratefulness is a spirit of contentment. This involves the ability to stop and enjoy the accomplishments of the family. If a father constantly urges his family on to more achievement and does not stop to enjoy what they have done, they will get discouraged and want to give up trying. They will feel they can never do enough to please him, so why try?

2. YOU MUST HAVE A GENUINE SPIRIT OF HUMILITY

- You must constantly remember that God is working with a fallible and weak person. Past failures are a key means of reminding yourself that there is no room for pride. Every father should maintain a "sanctified Hall of Shame" in the back of his mind. Whenever there is a tendency to be critical of a member of his family, he should mentally revisit his own "Hall of Shame."

- God has the right sort of jealousy. He will not share His glory with another. Whenever there is praise, the father must acknowledge that God is doing it and that it is only by His grace that things are working together.

- This humble spirit must carry over to those in your family. You must emphasize your need for your wife and each of your children. They need to hear you tell them that you need and love them. They need to hear that you can't do it yourself and that God never intended that. Emphasize that God brought you together as a team and that each one needs the other.

- A further aspect of humility must be demonstrated by you in admitting when you are wrong. If they do not see that you recognize your faults, they will immediately translate this as pride. They will also assume that you do not need them.

3. YOU MUST LEARN TO CONTROL YOUR TONGUE AND YOUR EMOTIONS

- A father does not have the right to be down emotionally. If he is down he should get up as quickly as possible. He cannot afford the luxury of wallowing in depression or complaining about how hard things are.

- The members of your family want to see in their father a consistency that they can count on. They become discouraged if they see their father up one day and down the next. They are expecting and needing continual encouragement and reassurance from him.

- By a man's words, he will be condemned and by his words, he will be justified. Harsh words and thoughtless statements cut deeply within the heart of a family member and are not easily removed. They fester like a cancer and produce a growing variety of complicated reactions to the father's leadership.

4. YOU MUST HAVE GOOD MANNERS

- The very essence of good manners involves continual sacrifice for the family. It involves yielding rights as Christ did. It is making sure that each one in the family is taken care of before the father meets his own needs.

- A father's manners demonstrate to the outside world what he really thinks about his wife and children.

- Lack of manners is a clear evidence to others that he does not respect his wife or children or cherish them as important people.
  A father's lack of manners will infect the family. His sons will develop a disrespect for their mother and their sisters. His wife and daughters will develop a devastating aloofness toward men.

5. YOU MUST ACCEPT EACH PERSON WHERE HE OR SHE IS

- A father must remember that every child has his or her own rate of development. He must give a balance of supervision and freedom to fail. Too much freedom will be interpreted by the children as rejection. Too much supervision will also be interpreted by the wife and children as rejection.

- A father must always remember where each child is going and be patient. He must also remember how far a child has come and be thankful. It is vital for a father to appreciate each person in the family for what they are now rather than what they might be in the future.

- A father should never compare anyone in his family with another person of greater ability or achievement. He can challenge the members of his family by exposing them to the lives of great Christians. This is different than the pressure of criticism by comparison.
The father must assure his children that he wanted them and that they are special provision from the Lord, just for that family.

- God is holding every father accountable for each child whom He entrusts to him.

6. A FATHER MUST RECOGNIZE INDIVIDUAL WORTH AND POTENTIAL

- A father must recognize the strong points and the weak points in each member of his family. He must emphasize the strong points and see how he could provide training which would strengthen the weak points.

- He must make a commitment to each person in the family that he is committed to their success and God's reputation rather than his reputation or the family's name.

- Family members need to be reassured that their father loves them and that, whether they are right or wrong, he always will love them. They can break his heart by doing evil, but they must sense that he will never disown them.

- A father must never ask members of a family to do things without expecting to give them more than what they have given. This is the unspoken commitment of a father. A father should not ask his family members to do things that he would not do.

- A father should anticipate that each member of his family is going to fail him at some time. He should, however, anticipate it and do all that he can to avoid it. If it is something that cannot be avoided, he must fortify them to go through it in victory.

- One clue to where a family member will fail is the weakness of a father in that same area. Scripture tells us that the sins of the parents are visited to the third and fourth generation. It is essential for a father to work out a program based on his own weaknesses. These should fortify his children against failure in the same area.

7. HE MUST EARN THE RIGHT TO BE HEARD

- No father should expect the right to be heard and he should certainly not demand it. He must earn this privilege by developing a relationship with each one in his family.

- Relationships take time and are fragile. Any discipline a father administers in the family must be on the basis of his relationship with that person. The basis of a father's commitment is to make them successful and to watch out for their safety. This requires continual sacrifice by him for each person in his family.

- When a father earns the right to be heard, he must cherish that right and not abuse it.

Special Note: Each one of the 30 Applications has been designed on the basis of a father earning the right to be heard. They allow the father to be in the position of a learner and a servant. This is the position that will achieve the greatest possible success.

☐ Study page 135.
☐ Complete Application No. 28.
☐ Define Quality No. 10 (page 6).

QUESTION No. 28

How can I learn to be gentle in the way I treat my wife and family?

ANSWER:

Gentleness is a fruit of God's Spirit. The more you grow to be "mighty in Spirit," the more you will become gentle in your words and actions. Gentleness is destroyed by pride and moral impurity. It is replaced by impatience and a judgmental spirit.

DO YOU KNOW HOW TO CONQUER A JUDGMENTAL SPIRIT?

☐ **Judging others reveals that we are guilty of the same thing. We have the same root sin, which may be demonstrated in a different way.**

☐ **God proves that we are guilty of the same root sin by allowing us to fail in a related or identical way.**[1]

☐ **To conquer a judgmental spirit, we must learn by God's grace how to see the relationship between what we judge in others, and what we are guilty of in our own lives.**[2]

QUIZ No. 28   CAN YOU MATCH THE SAME SINS WE JUDGE?

THE THINGS WE JUDGE IN OTHERS	THE ROOT SINS BEHIND THE ACTIONS WE JUDGE	THE SAME ROOT SINS IN US IF WE JUDGE
1. PRIDE	He exalts himself above the authority God gave to him.	A. ☐ We refuse to discipline our thought life when we judge.
2. ENVY	He desires to have that which belongs to someone else.	B. ☐ We violate God's command not to judge in order to expose evil.
3. STEALING	He takes what does not belong to him.	C. ☐ We take what does not belong to us when we judge.
4. BOASTING	He tries to make himself look better in the eyes of others.	D. ☐ We fail to take the time and effort to restore when we judge.
5. LAZINESS	He refuses to spend the time and effort to do what he should.	E. ☐ We desire to have the right to judge, which belongs to God.
6. SLANDERING	He speaks evil of others.	F. ☐ By cutting him down, we make ourself look better than him.
7. COMPROMISE	He violated God's standards in order to reach his goal.	G. ☐ We exalt ourselves above the authority of God's Word which forbids judging.
8. IMMORALITY	He failed to obey the promptings of the Holy Spirit.	H. ☐ We speak evil of the law of God when we judge.
9. GLUTTONY	He refused to discipline his physical appetite.	I. ☐ We forsake those we are to serve when we judge.
10. DISLOYALTY	He forsook the one he was supposed to have served.	J. ☐ We reject the promptings of God's Holy Spirit when we judge.

PROVIDE COPIES FOR YOUR FAMILY.

1. Romans 2:1.
2. Matthew 7:1-2; Romans 2:1.

APPLICATION No. 28

1. Purpose to be kind and gentle in the way that you treat your wife and children.

Lord, teach me "the meekness and gentleness of Christ."[1]

2. Determine what personal rights[2] cause you to be impatient and angry with your wife of children:

☐ The right to relax
☐ The right to a quiet house
☐ The right to good meals
☐ The right to spend your money

☐ The right to your possessions
☐ The right to be respected
☐ The right to be understood
☐ The right to a clean home

3. Yield all these personal rights to God. Expect God to test you in what you give to Him. Plan now to thank God if He does not allow you to enjoy one of these rights (as a privilege).

4. Discern the things which kill kindness and love.

PRIDE: "Only by pride cometh contention...."[3]
- Pride is reserving for yourself the right to make final decisions.
- Pride is believing that you achieved what God and others have done for you.
- Pride is standing in the position of God and judging your family.

MORAL IMPURITY: "He that soweth iniquity (moral impurity) shall reap vanity (spiritual emptiness) and the rod of his anger shall fail (*kalah:* utterly destroy)."[4]

- Impurity destroys the work of the Holy Spirit in your life.[5]
- Impurity destroys your love toward God and your family.[6]
- Impurity destroys your ability to give effective discipline.[4]
- Impurity destroys your sensitivity to the real needs of your wife and family.[7]

5. Apply the quiz on judging to yourself. Be ready to share some personal illustrations with your family when you give them the quiz. Give the right answer for each question before you go on to the next question.

ANSWERS:

1. (G) We exalt ourselves above the authority of God's Word which forbids judging (Matt. 7:1).
2. (E) We desire the right to judge which belongs to God (James 4:12).
3. (C) We take what does not belong to us when we judge (Romans 12:19).
4. (F) By cutting him down, we make ourselves look better than him (Isaiah 65:5).
5. (D) We fail to take the time and effort to restore when we judge (Galatians 6:1).
6. (H) We speak evil of the law of God when we judge (James 4:11).
7. (B) We violate God's command not to judge in order to expose evil (Matthew 7:1).
8. (J) We reject the promptings of God's Holy Spirit when we judge (John 7:24).
9. (A) We refuse to discipline our thought life when we judge (II Corinthians 10:4-5).
10. (I) We forsake those we are to serve when we judge (I Peter 2:16).

1. A personalization of II Corinthians 10:1.
2. Distinguish between personal rights and God-given responsibilities.
3. Proverbs 13:10.
4. Proverbs 22:8.
   Strong's Concordance.

5. Galatians 5:17.
6. Matthew 24:12.
7. Jude 10.

QUESTION No. 29

How can I teach my family to be grateful for all of the things that I do for them?

ANSWER:

You can teach your family to be grateful for all of the things that you do for them by learning how to be genuinely grateful for all the little things which your wife and children and parents do for you! The best way to teach gratefulness is to show gratefulness.

QUIZ No. 29   **CAN YOU PASS A TEST ON GRATEFULNESS?**

● In the next five minutes, how many people can you list who have benefited your life or family?

PEOPLE WHO HAVE BENEFITED MY LIFE SINCE I WAS BORN	SPECIFIC THINGS THEY HAVE DONE TO BENEFIT MY LIFE	HOW I HAVE THANKED THEM

PROVIDE COPIES FOR YOUR FAMILY.

APPLICATION No. 29

1. Purpose to teach your family how to be grateful by being genuinely grateful for the many things which they and others have done to enrich your life.

I will give thanks in all things, for this is your will in Christ Jesus for me.[1]

2. Privately take the gratefulness test on the opposite page. The lack of ability to remember those who benefited our lives is a clear evidence of a lack of gratefulness.

3. Fill in the first and second columns with the following helps:

☐ Mother...who brought you into the world and cared for you.
☐ Father...who worked to support the family and sacrificed for you.
☐ Grandparents...who enriched your life as you grew up.
☐ Pastors...who taught, counselled, and encouraged your parents.
☐ Pastors...who taught, counselled, and encouraged you.
☐ Christians...who prayed for you and exhorted you.
☐ Christians...who gave you an example by their lives.
☐ Friends...who provided a good influence for you and protected you.
☐ Neighbors...who benefited you or your family.
☐ Teachers...who taught you knowledge and skills.
☐ Doctors...who gave you medical care.
☐ Employers...who gave you jobs and training.
☐ People...who corrected you when you were wrong.
☐ People...who trusted you and defended your reputation.
☐ People...who worked for you and helped you to succeed.

4. Start to show gratefulness by choosing one person and taking the time and the effort to personally thank him or her.

☐ Explain how he or she has benefited your life and how grateful you are.
☐ Do it by letter, visit, or phone call. Would a gift be appropriate?
☐ Share your experience with your family as an introduction to the quiz.

5. Train yourself to increase gratefulness to your family.

☐ Find at least five things for which to thank God, your wife, and your children each day. Increase the number each week.
☐ Examples of things for which to thank your children:

☐ Time required to make hair attractive	☐ Cleaning the washbowl
☐ A cheerful smile	☐ Keeping in touch with relatives and friends.
☐ Washing dishes (deserves special thanks)	☐ Saving money on good buys
☐ Making meals	☐ Spending time with God.
☐ Taking out garbage	☐ Not being discouraged
☐ Washing, ironing.	☐ Wanting to talk to you.
☐ Cleaning home.	☐ Caring for children.
☐ Interest in decorating.	☐ Praying for you.

☐ Examples of things to thank your children for:

☐ Asking you a question.	☐ Obeying a command.
☐ Reading their Bible.	☐ Memorizing a verse.
☐ Care in appearance.	☐ Wise choice of friends.
☐ Good taste in music.	☐ Love for the Lord.
☐ Desire to witness.	☐ Telling the truth.
☐ Asking forgiveness.	☐ Praying for you.
☐ Forgiving family members.	☐ Praying before a meal.
☐ Going to church faithfully.	☐ Giving money to God.
☐ Being generous with others	☐ Sitting with you in church.

6. Remember that one of the basic functions of authority is "for the praise of them that do well."[3]

1. A personalization of I Thessalonians 5:18.   3. Romans 13:1-6.
2. I Peter 2:14.

☐ Study pages 146-147.
☐ Complete Application No. 30.
☐ Develop Quality No. 10 (page 6).
☐ Review this manual next year.

QUESTION No. 30

How can I learn to have genuine love for each one in my family?

ANSWER:

You can learn to have genuine love for each one in your family by meditating on God's definition of love and learning how to apply it to every thought, word, action, and attitude in your life.

WHAT IS GOD'S TEST OF GENUINE LOVE?[1]

1. <u>Love does not lose patience.</u> When did your husband show patience instead of getting angry?
   - ☐ When you misunderstood instructions.
   - ☐ When you disobeyed him.
   - ☐ When you caused an accident.
   - ☐ When you did something foolish.
   - ☐ When you showed disrespect.
   - ☐ When you disturbed his sleep.

2. <u>Love looks for ways to be kind and helpful.</u> How did your husband go out of his way to help you?
   - ☐ Helped you make a decision.
   - ☐ Helped you repair an item.
   - ☐ Helped you understand something.
   - ☐ Helped you with your work.

3. <u>Love is not envious or possessive.</u> How has your husband demonstrated contentment and generosity?
   - ☐ By avoiding extravagant buying.
   - ☐ By being grateful for what he has.
   - ☐ By dedicating his family to God.
   - ☐ By giving things cheerfully.

4. <u>Love is not eager to impress others.</u> When did your husband give honor to others that he could have accepted?
   - ☐ When he was praised for work.
   - ☐ When he rejected vain clothing.
   - ☐ When he was thanked for attitudes.
   - ☐ When he admitted his failures.

5. <u>Love is not puffed up or boastful.</u> How has your husband avoided inflated ideas of his own importance?
   - ☐ By not using exaggerations.
   - ☐ By asking for help when needed.
   - ☐ By listening more than talking.
   - ☐ By not thinking he is always right.

6. <u>Love has good manners.</u> What manners does your husband have regularly?
   - ☐ Open doors for you.
   - ☐ Open the car door for you.
   - ☐ Help you with your coat.
   - ☐ Seat you at the table.
   - ☐ Listen when you talk to him.
   - ☐ Tell you his schedule.
   - ☐ Serve himself last at the table.
   - ☐ Demonstrate good table manners.
   - ☐ Illustrate neatness at home.
   - ☐ Help you lift heavy items.

7. <u>Love does not pursue selfish advantage.</u> In what ways has your husband not insisted on his own rights?
   - ☐ By doing dishes.
   - ☐ By stopping conflicting hobbies.
   - ☐ By doing activities you choose.
   - ☐ By letting you use the washroom first.

8. <u>Love is not touchy or resentful.</u> When have you seen your husband overcome resentment?
   - ☐ When someone criticized him.
   - ☐ When someone ridiculed him.
   - ☐ When someone rejected him.
   - ☐ When someone misunderstood him.

1. I Corinthians 13:4-8.

APPLICATION No. 30

1. Purpose to concentrate on achieving more of God's genuine love.

That I might know the love of Christ which surpasses human knowledge.[1]

2. Ask your wife to write out the answers to this test on love.

3. Memorize the sixteen aspects of genuine love. Make them your life-long goals.

---

9. <u>Love does not keep account of evil.</u> **What offenses has your husband never reminded you about?**

☐ Making a foolish purchase. ☐ Ruining a good opportunity.
☐ Giving bad advice that he used. ☐ Violating God's moral standards.

10. <u>Love does not gloat over the wickedness of others.</u> **How has your husband not rejoiced in other's evil?**

☐ By not giving bad reports. ☐ By praying for them.
☐ By trying to restore them. ☐ By not comparing himself to them.

11. <u>Love rejoices when truth prevails.</u> **How has your husband rejoiced with you over truth?**

☐ Cleared his conscience. ☐ Helped me memorize Scripture.
☐ Helped me clear my conscience. ☐ Sought out Christian friends.

12. <u>Love welcomes pressures to test it.</u> **What pressures have tested your husband's love?**

☐ Rejection by loved ones. ☐ Tragedies in the family.
☐ Unexpected financial losses. ☐ Physical pain and sickness.

13. <u>Love believes the best.</u> **When has your husband demonstrated trust in you?**

☐ When you were falsely accused. ☐ When you arrived home late.
☐ When others misunderstood you. ☐ When you gave an appearance of evil.

14. <u>Love hopes for the gain of others.</u> **How has your husband demonstrated unfading hope?**

☐ Praying years for a person. ☐ Working to restore communication.
☐ Giving in spite of ungratefulness. ☐ Expecting God to glorify Himself.

15. <u>Love endures whatever is hurled against it.</u> **How has your husband shown endurance without weakening?**

☐ Thanking God for reverses. ☐ Sharing comfort learned in trials.
☐ Remaining cheerful in losses. ☐ Looking at heaven's joys.

16. <u>Love never fails.</u> **It still stands when all else has fallen.**

ANSWERS TO QUIZ PLACEMAT No. 30

Several answers could fit each question. Here are the most precise answers.

1. (F)	4. (I)	7. (H)	10. (E)
2. (A)	5. (L)	8. (G)	11. (D)
3. (K)	6. (J)	9. (B)	12. (C)

1. A personalization of Ephesians 3:19.

"...CONSIDER HIM THAT ENDURED...LEST YE BE WEARIED AND FAINT IN YOUR MINDS"

—a medical description

GOD'S GREATEST EXPRESSION OF LOVE

"Greater love hath no man than this, that a man lay down his life for his friends" (John 15:13).

If you are to truly love and make each member of your family successful, you must be willing to lay down your life on a daily basis and "die" for them. This means putting the needs of your family first, above your rights, personal ambitions, and schedule.

The greatest example of one laying down his life for his friends is Christ. We can never fully comprehend the spiritual aspect of Christ's suffering and shame, but medical studies shed glimpses of light on the physical agony and all the horror that Jesus endured on the cross.

"For consider Him that endured such contradiction of sinners against himself, let ye be wearied and faint in your minds" (Hebrews 12:3).

The physical trauma of Christ begins in Gethsemane with one of the initial aspects of his suffering—the bloody sweat. It is interesting that the physician of the group, St. Luke, is the only one to mention this. He says, "And being in agony, He prayed the longer. And his sweat became as drops of blood, trickling down upon the ground."

Though very rare, the phenomenon of Hematidrosis, or bloody sweat, is well documented. Under great emotional stress, tiny capillaries in the sweat glands can break, thus mixing blood with sweat. This process alone could have produced marked weakness and possible shock.

After the arrest in the middle of the night, Jesus was brought before the Sanhedrin and Caiaphas, the High Priest. A soldier struck Jesus across the face for remaining silent when questioned by Caiaphas. The palace guards then blindfolded Him and mockingly taunted Him to identify them as they each passed by, spat on Him, and struck Him in the face.

Condensed from "The Crucifixion of Jesus"
by C. Truman Davis, M.D., M.S.
March, 1965

In the early morning, Jesus, battered and bruised, dehydrated, and exhausted from a sleepless night, is taken across Jerusalem to the Praetorium of the Fortress Antonia. It was there, in response to the cries of the mob, that Pilate ordered Bar-Abbas released and condemned Jesus to scourging and crucifixion.

Preparations for the scourging are carried out. The prisoner is stripped of His clothing and His hands tied to a post above His head. The Roman legionnaire steps forward with the flagrum in his hand. This is a short whip consisting of several heavy, leather thongs with two small balls of lead attached near the ends of each. The heavy whip is brought down with full force again and again across Jesus' shoulders, back and legs.

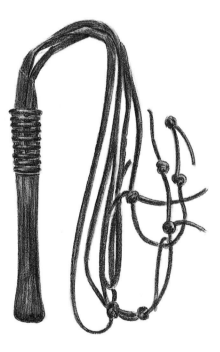

At first the heavy thongs cut through the skin only. Then, as the blows continue, they cut deeper into the subcutaneous tissues, producing first an oozing of blood from the capillaries and veins of the skin, and finally spurting arterial bleeding from vessels in the underlying muscles. The small balls of lead first produce large, deep bruises which are broken open by subsequent blows.

Finally the skin of the back is hanging in long ribbons and the entire area is an unrecognizable mass of torn, bleeding tissue. When it is determined by the centurion in charge that the prisoner is near death, the beating is finally stopped.

The half-fainting Jesus is then untied and allowed to slump to the stone pavement, wet with His own blood. The Roman soldiers see a great joke in this provincial Jew claiming to be a king. They throw a robe across His shoulders and place a stick in His hand for a scepter. A small bundle of flexible branches covered with long thorns is pressed into His scalp.

Again there is copious bleeding (the scalp being one of the most vascular areas of the body). After mocking Him and striking Him across the face, the soldiers take the stick from His hand and strike Him across the head, driving the thorns deeper into His scalp. Finally, they tire of their sadistic sport and the robe is torn from His back. This had already become adherent to the clots of blood and serum in the wounds, and its removal, just as in the careless removal of a surgical bandage, causes excruciating pain—almost as though He were again being whipped, and the wounds again begin to bleed.

The heavy beam of the cross is then tied across His shoulders, and the procession of the condemned Christ, two thieves and the execution detail, begins its slow journey. The weight of the heavy wooden beam, together with the shock produced by copious blood loss, is too much. He stumbles and falls. The rough wood of the beam gouges into the lacerated skin and muscles of the shoulders. He tries to rise, but human muscles have been pushed beyond their endurance.

At Golgotha, the beam is placed on the ground and Jesus is quickly thrown backward with His shoulders against the wood. The legionnaire feels for the depression at the front of the wrist. He drives a heavy, square, wrought-iron nail through the wrist and deep into the wood. Quickly, he moves to the other side and repeats the action, being careful not to pull the arms too tightly, but to allow some flexion and movement. The beam is then lifted in place at the top of the posts and the titulus reading "Jesus of Nazareth, King of the Jews" is nailed in place.

The left foot is pressed backward against the right foot, and with both feet extended, toes down, a nail is driven through the arch of each. As He pushes Himself upward to avoid the stretching torment, He places His full weight on the nail through His feet. Again there is the searing agony of the nail tearing through the nerves between the metatarsal bones of the feet.

As the arms fatigue, great waves of cramps sweep over the muscles, knotting them in deep, relentless, throbbing pain. With these cramps comes the inability to push Himself upward. Hanging by His arms, the pectoral muscles are paralyzed and the intercostal muscles are unable to act. Air can be drawn into the lungs, but cannot be exhaled. Jesus fights to raise Himself in order to get even one short breath. Finally, carbon dioxide builds up in the lungs and in the blood stream and the cramps partially subside. Spasmodically, He is able to push Himself upward to exhale and bring in the life-giving oxygen.

Hours of this limitless pain, cycles of twisting, joint-rending cramps, intermittent partial asphyxiation, searing pain as tissue is torn from His lacerated back as He moves up and down against the rough timber. Then another agony begins. A deep crushing pain deep in the chest as the pericardium slowly fills with serum and begins to compress the heart.

The compressed heart is struggling to pump heavy, thick, sluggish blood into the tissues—the tortured lungs are making a frantic effort to gasp in small gulps of air. The markedly dehydrated tissues send their flood of stimuli to the brain. Jesus gasps, "I thirst."

He can feel the chill of death creeping through His tissues. With one last surge of strength, He once again presses His torn feet against the nail, straightens His legs, takes a deeper breath, and utters His seventh and last cry, "Father, into thy hands I commit my spirit."

Apparently to make doubly sure of death, the legionnaire drove his lance through the fifth interspace between the ribs, upward through the pericardium and into the heart. Immediately there came out blood and water. We, therefore, have rather conclusive post-mortem evidence the Our Lord died, not the usual crucifixion death by suffocation, but of heart failure due to shock and constriction of the heart by fluid in the pericardium.

"And let us not be weary in well doing: for in due season we shall reap, if we faint not" (Galatians 6:9).

INDEX

Listing of names, places, and selected words from Manual contents. Bold numerals indicate illustrations.

INDEX OF SCRIPTURAL REFERENCES

QUESTION INDEX

ALIENATED SONS AND DAUGHTERS

APATHY TOWARD MEDITATION

DEALING WITH TEMPTATIONS

DECEPTION THROUGH FALSE PHILOSOPHIES

DESTRUCTIVE ARGUMENTS

DISRESPECT (IRREVERENCE) FOR GOD'S WORD

CONFLICTING PRIORITIES

DIFFICULT DECISIONS WITH SONS AND DAUGHTERS

DISINTEREST IN MEMORIZATION

DISSATISFIED WIVES AND CHILDREN

DOUBTS ABOUT THE BIBLE

HARMFUL INFLUENCES IN THE HOME

HINDRANCES TO EFFECTIVE LEADERSHIP

INSENSITIVITY TO SPIRITUAL DANGERS

LACK OF CONVICTIONS

MISUNDERSTANDINGS ABOUT GRACE

NEED FOR GODLY HEROES

NEED TO BE "MIGHTY IN SPIRIT"

NEGLECT OF GOD'S WORD

PAST FAILURE

PROBLEMS IN DECISION MAKING

RESPONSIBILITY FOR DISCIPLINE

SELF-REJECTION

UNWISE FRIENDSHIPS

M.M. Vol.I-C 6-80-50M